Noreen Mackey

The Crystal Fountain

THE STORY OF AN INNER JOURNEY

the columba press

First published in 2007 by

the columba press

55A Spruce Avenue, Stillorgan Industrial Park,
Blackrock, Co Dublin

Cover by Bill Bolger
Origination by The Columba Press
Printed in Ireland by ColourBooks Ltd, Dublin

ISBN 978 1 85607 567 1

Author's Acknowledgements

Thanks to all those who helped in any way to bring this book into being. To Brendan Walsh and Rosemary O'Loughlin, who read early drafts and made suggestions which greatly improved the final product; to Liz Heffernan for advice and affirmation; to Seán O Boyle and the staff at Columba for the finished product; to Bill Bolger for a wonderful cover design. And thanks in a special way to the many fellow travellers that I met (and continue to meet), who keep me company along the way. It's good to know that you're there.

Copyright Acknowledgements

Biblical quotations are in the New Revised Standard Version, copyright © 1989 by the Division of Christian Education of the National Council of the Churches of Christ in the United States of America. All rights reserved. Used by permission. Quotations from John of the Cross are from *The Complete Works of John of the Cross* translated by E. Allison Peers, and are used by kind permission of Burns & Oates, a division of The Continuum Publishing Group, London.

www.noreenmackey.com

For Finbarr Lynch SJ, anam-chara,
and to the memory of Sean O'Leary, judge of
the High Court, who died on 22 December 2006.

Likewise the Spirit helps us in our weakness; for we do not know how to pray as we ought, but that very Spirit intercedes with sighs too deep for words. And God, who searches the heart, knows what is the mind of the Spirit, because the Spirit intercedes for the saints according to the will of God.

Romans 8:26-27

CHAPTER ONE

Whither hast thou hidden thyself,
and hast left me, O Beloved, to my sighing?
Thou didst flee like the hart, having wounded me:
I went out after thee, calling, and thou wert gone.

The little oratory in the guesthouse of the great Abbey of Chambarand was silent and peaceful. From where I stood just inside the door, I could see whitewashed walls, some pine prayer stools and two or three rush-bottomed chairs. A sanctuary lamp glowed before a small brass tabernacle and the low evening sun of early September, slanting through the stained glass of the west windows, spilled pools of colour onto the polished wooden floor. The still air was heavy with the smell of candle wax and floor-polish. It was a simple, uncluttered place; a place where a person might catch her breath and begin to revive again a little.

I moved forward and bent down to look at the large leather-covered bible that lay open on a red velvet cushion at the base of the tabernacle. 'And being in agony,' I read, 'He prayed the longer.' Someone had left the book open at the account of the agony of Jesus in the Garden of Gethsemane, and my own sense of desolation eased a little as I thought of his at that moment when even his friends could not stay awake to keep watch with him in face of the horror that was lurking.

Only two hours earlier, I had arrived at the Trappistine Abbey of Chambarand in the French Alps where I was to spend the following two weeks. I had been travelling since early morning, a long train journey that had taken me across France from Aubépine to Lyon, from Lyon to Valence and from Valence to St-Marcellin, where I had been met by the local taxi-cum-ambulance and driven the remaining few kilometres to the Abbey. But the inner journey I had made that day was still longer. That morning, I had been Sister Noreen-Marie de Jésus, a novice in

the Carmel of Aubépine, but the journey I had made in the intervening hours had been so long that Sister Noreen-Marie no
longer existed. I was not that novice. I was Noreen Mackey, erst-
while lawyer and now homeless unemployed person.

The leaving of Aubépine had been devastating, for I had left
against my will. I had joined the little community of eighteen
nuns a year and a half earlier, convinced that it was where I was
supposed to be for the rest of my life. Three years before, while
working as a lawyer with the European Court of Justice in
Luxembourg, I had read a verse of a poem that had caused me to
embark upon a quest for union with God. The quest had led me
to Aubépine, thinking that there I would find the secret place
where God dwelt. But it was soon clear to everyone around me,
if not to myself, that the way of life of a Carmelite nun was not
for me. Difficulty piled on difficulty, misunderstanding climbed
on the back of misunderstanding, until after a dramatic show-
down with the mistress of novices in which I had exhibited all
the petulance of a prima donna being invited to join the chorus, I
was asked to leave.

The place I had now come to was a high place, a plateau on
the right bank of the river Isère, six hundred metres above sea
level. There the Abbey rose from the surrounding woods and
pasturelands to dominate the countryside like a great eagle
upon its nest. Chambarand was not by any means one of the
older Trappist abbeys, having been built only in the second half
of the nineteenth century. The first nuns had come there from
the Abbey of Sept-Fons, but had been obliged to leave again in
1903, driven out by the anti-clerical laws in force in France at that
time. Not until 1931 did the Trappistines return to Chambarand.

The oratory where I was standing was in the New
Guesthouse. The Abbey *hôtellerie* comprised two quite separate
buildings. One, the Old Guesthouse, was full at the time of my
arrival, so I found myself the sole occupant of the new building.
Sister Gloria, who had met me on my arrival, had brought me
there, to a small white room on the first floor.

Sister Gloria was not at all what I had expected a Trappistine in a French abbey to be like. First of all, disconcertingly, she was English. Sixty-ish, brisk and efficient, with a decisive manner and clipped vowels, she brought to mind the headmistress of a girl's boarding school. When I was no longer in her company, I tended to think of her as wearing a twin-set and pearls, so that it came as something of a shock, each time I met her, to see her dressed in the black and white habit of her order.

The dining room was in the Old Guesthouse. At my first meal, on the evening of my arrival, about twenty guests were seated around a long refectory table and the room was a babble of conversation. The meal was served by the guest-mistress, Sister Thérèse Agnès, a tall, thin, dark-haired, no-nonsense sort of person, of whom I felt slightly scared. A little overwhelmed at meeting so many new people all at once, I kept my head down and my attention on my plate for the first twenty minutes. After that, finding that nobody was taking any notice of me, I began to look around at the other guests.

A man who seemed to be alone was sitting on my left. I had been aware of him since I sat down. Something in his manner grated: it was too sudden, too abrupt. He pulled his chair up to the table roughly, so that its legs made a loud scraping sound on the tiled floor. His fork clattered to his plate between mouthfuls. Up to this he hadn't spoken to anyone, but had concentrated on his food with such single-minded attention that he was filling his plate for the third time before anyone else had arrived at the point of second helpings. He seemed to be hungry. Now he suddenly noticed me.

'Are you a pilgrim?' he demanded abruptly, leaning towards me and breathing fumes of garlic into my face.

Taken aback and recoiling a little, I said that I wasn't.

'I am,' he said. 'I spend my whole life on pilgrimage. I'm resting here for a few days before I go on again.'

Something about the way he spoke jarred, but I couldn't quite put my finger on what it was. I looked at him more closely. He looked as if he was in his forties or fifties, hair thinning but still dark; wrinkled skin nut-brown from exposure to the sun.

His pale blue eyes burned with a fanatical light, and as he fixed them on me now and continued to speak, I suddenly realised what was strange about his speech. He was addressing me with the familiar *tu* instead of the more usual *vous*. I had become sensitive to the nuances of the French language over the past few years, and felt ridiculously offended to be addressed so familiarly by a stranger. I decided to put a stop to it immediately.

'Where are you going on pilgrimage?' I asked him.

Vous. That usually worked. The last time I had been obliged to resort to such a tactic was on the beach in Nice some seven or eight years previously, with gratifying results. The over-friendly and rather importunate man in question had reacted as if I had slapped him on the face.

It didn't seem to be working now. The pilgrim took no offence at all.

'I go everywhere,' he said expansively. 'I have just come from La Salette. I haven't made up my mind yet where I will go next. But it doesn't matter. I am a pilgrim, you see (*tu!*), and so I am always on pilgrimage. It is what I do. I go from shrine to shrine, and I sleep in monasteries along the way. I am welcomed everywhere because I am a pilgrim. I can sleep in all the monasteries for free,' he added.

I had never met a professional pilgrim before. There were a lot of things I wanted to know, but I couldn't think of a polite way to enquire. Had he set out in life to become a pilgrim, as a result, for example, of a religious experience? Or was his pilgrimly state a reaction to circumstances? Had he found himself, for whatever reason, without a home and a job? Had he decided to turn his homelessness to a spiritual use? Suddenly, I felt embarrassed, and wished I hadn't made the little *vous* and *tu* fuss. I thought of the courage and will-power it must take to decide to keep on the move, and to give it a point, instead of just drifting. I thought of St Benedict Joseph Labré, another Frenchman, who dressed in rags and was taken by everyone for a beggar and a down-and-out. This man beside me might be just such a person. What did I know, anyway? I should have learned by now that you cannot judge anyone by appearance. I was reminded of a remarkable woman I had once met in the *hôtellerie* at Aubépine. Her name was Lydia, and when I met her, she was in her early seventies. Some thirty years earlier she had read one day the passage from the gospel where Jesus tells his disciples to go out without shoes or purse or haversack, and she felt directly addressed. She was at the time (and still was when I met her) a member of the Congregation of the Little Sisters of Jesus, whose members live and work among the underprivileged and the marginalised. She got the reluctant permission of her superior to answer what seemed to her to be her calling, and she set out to wander the roads of Europe, without money, carrying just one change of clothes and a bible in a knapsack, sleeping at night wherever she could get shelter. If she was refused shelter in one house, she knocked at another door, and if she could find no shelter at all she slept in the open. She spent her days walking and in prayer, totally without fear or anxiety, a living witness to all who met her of God's care for those who trust absolutely in him. She was one of the happiest people I have ever met.

One day, I asked her what would happen if her family needed to get in touch with her urgently, and she answered in matter-of-fact tones that God would arrange it. To illustrate the point, she told me that she had once been taken suddenly ill, just as she arrived at a village where there was a house of her congregation. Realising that she would have to rest, she called at the convent, where the sisters were overcome with relief to see her. They had just received word that her father had been taken seriously ill, and they were in a great state because nobody knew where Lydia was. And then she walked in. Just like that! So she was able to go to her father, who died shortly after her arrival, while she was with him.

Lydia was a highly entertaining companion, full of an almost medieval faith in God's providence but full too of hilarious tales of her travels. One in particular gives a flavour of the sort of woman she was. It was her habit when arriving in a town or village towards night-fall to knock at the first door she came to and ask for '*un petit place*' for the night. 'I'm small,' she explained to me, 'I don't take up much space, so I only need a little place.'

Finding herself one night in a town in Italy, she knocked first at the door of a convent. A young nun answered, and surveyed with some surprise this tiny grey-haired woman, rucksack on back, wearing baggy blue cotton trousers and with a blue cotton scarf tied around her head. Not speaking much Italian, Lydia attempted to translate her need for *un petit place* into that language. She knew that the Italian word for *place* was *post*, and she also knew that Italians created diminutives by adding *ino* or *ina* to a noun. It seemed very simple.

'Please,' she said to the young nun, 'I badly need a *postino* for the night. Just one night will be enough for me.'

The look of utter horror that greeted this simple request puzzled her greatly. Only when the Mother Superior was called to deal with the crisis did Lydia discover that *postino* is the Italian for 'postman'…

When I met her, she had been walking for some days with an injured foot. She spent two days in Aubépine, just to give the foot a rest, and my last sight of her was of a tiny figure hobbling off across a cornfield towards a distant wood, on the next leg of her unending journey.

Thinking of her now, I looked with new eyes at the pilgrim. Who knew what his personal history had been? What mysteries all of us are! Each of us sitting around that table was mysterious in a different way: the aristocratic-looking elderly lady with the dangling earrings opposite me, the young girl who sat beside her and who, head bent, lank dark hair falling over her face and almost dipping into her food, was shovelling pasta into her mouth with the rapidity and single-mindedness of a small dog, glancing furtively around now and again from under her lashes and dropping her eyes hastily if she encountered a glance. There was a story behind each one: some different reason had brought each of us to that table in the Abbey of Chambarand on that night of the eighth of September, 1997.

To my right sat a comfortable-looking, middle-aged couple.

From the ease and familiarity with which they addressed one another, I took it that they were either husband and wife or brother and sister. The man was grey-haired and amiable, dressed in pale slacks and a yellow polo shirt. He could have been a university professor or a teacher in a *lycée*. The woman was doing most of the talking. She was voluble and enthusiastic, her tightly permed silver head nodding vigorously to emphasis the points she was making. Having noticed my accent when I spoke to the pilgrim, she now introduced herself as Paule and asked me where I was from. I told her I was Irish.

'And what brings someone all the way from Ireland to Chambarand?' Paule asked politely.

I had anticipated this question, and had a prepared answer. I had no desire to get into the history of my recent abortive attempt at the religious life.

'I've been working for some years in Luxembourg,' I told her. 'My contract has now ended, and I'm between jobs.'

This was not untrue; it just discounted entirely the past eighteen months. Now Paule told me that her youngest daughter was at present doing a *stage* in the abbey, with a view to joining the community later on. Her *stage* was drawing to a close and Paule and her husband François had come to spend a few days there and bring her back to Paris with them. Her daughter seemed happy, Paule said. She and François had felt very anxious about the whole thing, but having met the abbess and the novice-mistress, they were somewhat reassured.

This nice couple had, of course, no idea of the effect this information had on me. I was suddenly overcome by an almost unbearable mixture of emotions: envy of the unknown young woman who was starting out on the same adventure I had embarked on with such hope two years earlier; sadness and bitterness at the way my own attempt had ended; anxiety and uncertainty about what to do next and, over it all, a vast and all-encompassing home-sickness for Aubépine. Making a hurried excuse, I left the table, my meal unfinished. I felt like someone who was standing on narrow, rocky promontory. Before me lay a vast, grey expanse of ocean; behind me, the waves were slowly washing the earth away, creating an abyss, cutting off my return. There was nowhere I could go but forward, but I could see no land. My desolation knew no bounds.

CHAPTER TWO

Shepherds, ye that go
yonder, through the sheepcotes, to the hill,
If perchance ye see him that I most love,
tell ye him that I languish, suffer and die.

Aubépine! I simply could not believe that I would never see it again. What had gone wrong? I was convinced that my departure had been a terrible mistake. I could see no other future. I wanted to live a life of prayer and contemplation, but how could I do it without the support and structure of life in a community of like-minded people? Everything that had taken place in my life during the previous four and a half years was thrown into question, including – indeed, above all – the relationship I believed I had with God. In Luxembourg, I thought I had experienced a call to give my life to God in a total way; now it seemed I was wrong. But I had built everything on that belief: I had given up my job at the European Court, the apartment I loved in Luxembourg, a lifestyle that was pleasant and comfortable. And for what? For a fantasy, it now began to seem to me. If I had been wrong in thinking that God had called me to give my life to him, then it was more than likely that I had also been wrong in believing he had re-entered my life in Luxembourg. I thought again, with anguish now, of that summer night on my balcony when I had picked up a book and read the lines:

Whither hast thou hidden thyself, and hast left me,
O Beloved, to my sighing?
Thou didst flee like the hart, having wounded me:
I went out after thee, calling, and thou wert gone.

I thought I had experienced a sort of epiphany that night, and that thought had carried me all the way to Aubépine, and through some dark days there. Now I didn't know what to believe. Had it all been imagination? I was standing on the edge of an abyss that gave onto a void. For the moment I couldn't bear to even consider the possibility that there was nothing where I had thought there was everything.

My first steps away from the void were taken along the path of denial. I was right, I had to be: it was the nuns who had got it wrong. They had thrown the whole project into jeopardy. That had to be changed. So that first night in Chambarand, I wept and pleaded on the phone with Véronique, the prioress of Aubépine and Marie-Jeanne, the novice-mistress, to let me come back. Deeply distressed themselves, they nevertheless remained inflexible. I would have to accept that I did not belong in Aubépine, Véronique said firmly, reminding me of the stress that trying to live there had caused me. Finally, weary from crying and arguing, I ended the phone call and returned to my room to go to bed.

The room they had given me in the guesthouse was a pleasant one, small and well furnished in pale colours. It looked out onto a courtyard where the abbey cats sunned themselves all day long, and where from time to time, a workman from the abbey farm appeared to sit in the sun and smoke a cigarette. It was a peaceful room; I liked it and I felt safe there. While I was in that room, I could almost persuade myself that I was back in my cell at Aubépine; the cell that looked out upon the woods and fields that I would never see again. During the first few days at Chambarand, I only left my room for meals or to go to services in the abbey church.

Oh, that church! It was a huge, bleak, grey place, with a chilly, clammy atmosphere that grabbed at your bones. It must have been miserably cold in winter. It was also badly in need of redecoration. However, what the church lacked in aesthetic appeal was made up by the beauty of the services and the singing of the nuns. Their day began early. At four every morning, they rose to sing the office of vigils, although during the two weeks I spent there, I never managed to get up in time to attend it. Indeed, for the first few days I felt so exhausted that I didn't even get up for Mass at seven. On about the third day, I discovered there was a second Mass at ten-thirty, celebrated by an old retired priest who lived at the abbey. From then on I attended that Mass, which had the added advantage of having no other members of the public present, for I was finding it very difficult to be with other people during those first days away from Aubépine. I felt a misfit everywhere. Emotionally drained from all the conflicting emotions and stresses I had undergone during the previous weeks, I had no energy for anything. Apart from that, I never knew when something was going to suddenly reduce me to tears; so that, all in all, social contact was very wearing. Véronique, during her daily phone calls, kept trying to encourage me to go for walks in the beautiful countryside around the abbey; I did try once or twice, but felt lost, as though I had landed on an alien planet. Only in my room or in the little oratory did I feel safe during those early days.

It was on the fourth or fifth day that, thanks to Sister Gloria, I discovered the veranda. When I emerged from my room one morning, I found her on her knees on the stairs, sweeping them with a hand-brush. She greeted me with her usual friendliness, and asked if I had explored the guesthouse. I hadn't, lacking any more enthusiasm for this than for anything else.

'Come along,' she said briskly, clearly impatient with all this moping around, 'I'll give you a quick tour.'

It was in this way that I found out there was a small kitchen for the use of us guests, where we could make a cup of tea or coffee at any time. After Sister Gloria had returned to her sweeping, I went back to the kitchen and poked around a bit. Teabags, coffee and sugar were in jars in a cupboard, an electric kettle sat on the worktop, there was milk in the fridge and oh, joy of joys, there was a tin well stocked with biscuits! The heavy blue curtains on the window were closed. I drew them back, and there was the veranda, a paved, peaceful haven looking out over the abbey fields. Hurrying back upstairs I grabbed a book and ran back down again, almost afraid my treasure might have disappeared while I was away. But no, the veranda was still there. I boiled some water, made coffee in a blue pottery mug, put some biscuits on a plate, dragged a wicker chair and a small table from the kitchen onto the veranda and installed myself. The

September fields were drowsy and golden. The heavy heat of August had finally lifted, and the early autumn days were like those of high summer in Ireland. For the first time in months I relaxed and felt that it was good to be alive. The veranda was the nearest thing I had found yet to the balcony of my old apartment in Luxembourg and, sitting there, I was briefly happy.

Breakfast at Chambarand took place between eight and eight-forty. On the morning after my arrival, I made my way into the dining room about eight-fifteen. The only other person there was the young girl I had seen at dinner the previous evening. She was hunched over her cereal and didn't look up when I came in.

'Bonjour!' I tried.

She glanced at me briefly from under her eyelashes and muttered something incomprehensible. She didn't seem to want company, so I decided to leave her alone. A few more people came in while I was having breakfast, and there was some desultory conversation in which the young girl took no part. She brightened up only once, and that was when Sister Thérèse Agnès came in with a small dish of raspberries and presented them to her.

'A present for you, Colette,' she said, her rather authoritarian air considerably softened.

Colette's face lit up as she took the dish of fruit and looked up at the nun. I was puzzled by her reaction, which seemed out of proportion to the modesty of the gift. Shortly afterwards, the mystery was solved. All the guests were helping to wash up after breakfast, Colette included. Head bowed, face concealed by her hair, she took plates from those who were washing without making eye contact and dried them with her back turned to the company. François, Paule's husband, was trying hard to engage her in conversation, receiving for the most part monosyllabic replies. Finally,

'Have you been here long?' he asked her.

'*Je suis à l'abri ici,*' Colette replied, and all became clear to me. *Je suis à l'abri ici* – 'I am being sheltered here.' I had heard before of the system in France whereby some religious houses provided a sheltered environment for vulnerable persons. Colette then was one of these. Here was another person in pain. My heart warmed to Sister Thérèse Agnès who, up to this, I had found a bit intimidating, but who had obviously managed to find a place in Colette's affections.

As the days wore on, I tried to come to terms with my own feelings. Apart from experiencing a disturbing mixture of anger, bitterness and grief, I found prayer painful in a way unknown until now. I didn't know what posture to take, or how to be before God. This difficulty had a number of causes. First of all, I was in a state of anger and resentment towards Véronique and Marie-Jeanne in Aubépine. But added to that was guilt – guilt that I hadn't lived up to what I believed was my vocation and that somehow I hadn't made enough of an effort. It was true that, when I tried to pin this down, I couldn't see where I could have made a greater effort than I had done, but this did nothing to relieve the constant nagging guilt. In part, this was caused by the fact that I had nothing to show for my efforts. They had never resulted in success, so how could I test whether they were genuine? I thought of the occasions when Marie-Jeanne wanted me to do something that I didn't want to do: my face would freeze, despite the huge efforts I made to smile at her. A weight used to descend on my heart, a weight that seemed to paralyse my ability to behave in accordance with my undoubtedly good intentions. St Paul understood the dilemma well.

> For I know that nothing good dwells within me, that is, in my flesh. I can will what is right, but I cannot do it. For I do not do the good I want, but the evil I do not want is what I do... So I find it to be a law that when I want to do right, evil lies close at hand. For I delight in the law of God in my inmost self, but I see in my members another law at war with the law of my mind and making me captive to the law of sin which dwells in my members. Wretched man that I am! Who will deliver me from this body of death? (Romans 7:18-19; 21-24)

But below all these feelings was something I was afraid to look at too closely, that abyss whose edge I was standing on, that possibility that I had been the victim of one huge illusion from the start. If it was true, it would mean that God had never called me in any particular way. That opened up an even more appalling vista: the possibility that God took no special interest in me at all, or in anybody else for that matter. Since the whole of my life had been based on the contrary premise, I was afraid even to think what this would mean. For the moment, I turned my head away whenever that gaping void threatened to emerge from the surrounding fog.

One day, wandering aimlessly about the grounds of the abbey, I went into the abbey shop. This was an interesting place, a sort of Aladdin's cave of religious artefacts and books, smelling strongly of the cheese for which the abbey was famous. Browsing through a box of postcards of the abbey and its surroundings, intending to send some to family and friends, I came across a small card with nothing on it but a prayer surrounded by a design of yellow and blue flowers. It was entitled simply: *Prière de Charles de Foucauld*. I had of course heard before of the Vicomte de Foucauld, sometimes known as the Hermit of Tamanrasset – a French nobleman born in the late nineteenth century. Following a religious conversion, he had become a hermit in Algeria where he was killed in an anti-French uprising on 1 December 1916. The prayer on the card was short and simple. It said:

Father,
I abandon myself into your hands;
do with me what you will.
Whatever you may do, I thank you:
I am ready for all, I accept all.
Let only your will be done in me, and in all your creatures
– I wish no more than this, O Lord.
Into your hands I commend my soul:
I offer it to you with all the love of my heart,
for I love you, Lord, and so need to give myself,
to surrender myself into your hands without reserve,

and with boundless confidence,
for you are my Father.
Amen.

This prayer spoke to me in a way that nothing else had done during the previous weeks. It said everything that I wanted to say to God, for which I had been unable to find the words. Forgetting about the postcards I wanted to send, I paid for the little card and hurried from the shop, clutching it like a talisman.

Back in my room, I studied it more closely. I began to see that I could pray this prayer no matter what the reality of my situation. It seemed to me that there were only two possible reasons why I was no longer in Aubépine: either I had failed to live up to my vocation, and so was to blame for losing the pearl of great price, or I had been mistaken from the start in thinking that I had a vocation at all.

If the first reason was correct, then I was no longer where God wanted me to be. In that case, what could I do to remedy things? It seemed to me that the best I could do would be to abandon myself absolutely to his will in the terms of this prayer, and trust that he would draw good from evil. I remembered a verse of a poem written by St Thérèse of Lisieux:

L'Amour, j'en ai l'expérience
Du bien, du mal qu'il trouve en moi
Sait profiter (quelle puissance)
Il transforme mon âme en soi.
(Glose sur le Divin)

('I know from experience that Love, whether it finds good things or bad in me, is able to turn everything to profit; it transforms me into itself.')

So, I reasoned, even if I had done something wrong, God could – and would – draw good from it, if only I handed myself over completely to him. If, on the other hand, I had simply been mistaken from the start, then I could not go wrong now in abandoning myself completely to God and trusting that he would bring me to wherever it was that I should be. There was a sense of rest

21

fulness in handing things over in this way, although a careful reading of the prayer will show that abandonment is not a relinquishing of responsibility: 'Whatever you may do, I thank you: I am ready for all, I accept all' is easier to say than to live out. Nevertheless, for the first time in weeks I could see a small part of the path ahead, and I began to venture out just a short distance from the bleak and desolate place where I had been.

In this way, the two weeks in Chambarand passed for the most part in a sort of blur of grey misery, broken intermittently by a brief ray of daylight. Once or twice, the daylight even became sunlight. One of these sunny moments occurred towards the end of the first week. A new guest had come to stay at the abbey, a young woman who was a restorer of old paintings. Over dinner, she told us that she was working in the basilica at the nearby town of St-Antoine, where a fourteenth-century mural had been discovered hidden under plaster and paintings from a later period. She was attempting to uncover the entire mural, and she invited us to come and see the work in progress. St-Antoine was some distance from Chambarand and there was no public transport on the route, so I was delighted when Paule and François told me they were planning to drive there and invited me to go with them.

The outing to St-Antoine was my first excursion outside the walls of the abbey and indeed, my first real outing since I had entered Aubépine a year and a half previously. I had, it is true, attended a gathering of Carmelite novices in Lisieux, but that had merely been a transfer of the monastic life from one place to another. This was different; this was more like the sightseeing I had been used to of old, and I woke up that morning with an unaccustomed feeling of pleasurable excitement. Surprised, I realised that I was actually looking forward to something.

Paule and François were good travelling companions. They told me a little about their life in Paris, and about their daughter who was doing the *stage* at Chambarand. They had spoken to her that morning, and she had told them that her decision had been made; she would enter at Pentecost the following year. I could see that they were anxious about it; she was a girl with many friends and an active social life, and they wondered how she would feel when she could no longer leave the confines of the abbey. They were uneasy to about the heavy manual work the nuns did: their daughter wasn't used to work like that, they said. Listening to all of this, I didn't feel that it was the right moment to tell them that I had just left an enclosed monastery, and that the things they were worried about were among the things I had found most difficult.

It was a lovely late-summer day. That September was almost as warm as June, although without the heavy, stifling heat of my last few weeks at Aubépine, and the drive to St-Antoine took us along still-leafy lanes where the black and white cattle of the region viewed our progress contemplatively over the ditches and gates. When we arrived at the town, we went straight to the basilica, where we found our fellow-guest perched on a scaffold in front of the mural she was uncovering. It was a Virgin and Child, its colours so faded that it was almost impossible to distinguish them from one another. The young woman was painstakingly removing layers of paint and plaster, centimetre by centimetre. It was incredibly delicate work, as the least false movement could damage the original beyond repair. While we were there she uncovered another tiny portion of one of the virgin's hands, and it was a thrilling moment. Ours were the first eyes to see that hand in heaven knew how many centuries.

Eventually we left the basilica and went for a stroll around the town. St-Antoine is a town of artists, and their studios were everywhere. We wandered in and out, looking at the paintings, before finding a café for lunch. Sitting in the sun in an ivy-covered courtyard, sipping *vin rosé* and eating *salade niçoise*, I allowed myself to be taken over by the totally pleasurable sensations of wine on the palate and sun on the skin. I closed my eyes and emptied my mind. I felt totally relaxed; this was like the old days, and I didn't want it to end. But of course it had to, and as we drove back at last through the deepening dusk, my spirits sank again. My time in Chambarand was running out, and I had no job. Through the community in Aubépine I had arranged to rent an apartment in Metz while looking for work in Luxembourg. I hadn't seen the apartment. I had no idea what my future home was like, although I would be moving in there in less than a week. I had tried to avoid thinking about the future since my arrival in Chambarand, but the time was approaching when I would have to face it. It was daunting. I was forty-nine years old; I had no job, no permanent home. Above all, the horrible spectre that lay in wait for my unguarded moments was ever ready with its insidious suggestion that the whole foundation on which I had constructed my life was made of water. Had God ever called me at all, it whispered? Did God even care? Behind that question lurked an even more terrifying one, but that was where the true void lay and I would not go there.

CHAPTER THREE

Seeking my love
I will go o'er yonder mountains and banks;
I will neither pluck the flowers nor fear the wild beasts;
I will pass by the mighty and cross the frontiers.

September was almost over and the low evening sun shone down upon the Rue Chimay. Directly across the street from where I was sitting in the window of my hotel I could see the façade of Peter Pin, the furniture shop where I had bought a desk for my apartment two years earlier. I was back in Luxembourg, a place I had never expected to see again, the place where it had all begun. A week earlier, I had left Chambarand and gone to Metz, as planned. The apartment the nuns had found for me there was lovely: three rooms on the ground floor of a wonderful old house set in a large overgrown garden. Mademoiselle Martin, the owner of the house, a single woman of 'a certain age' as they say kindly in France to describe anyone over forty, was a remarkable woman whose acquaintance I would in any other circumstances have been delighted to make (and indeed, I happily renewed it some months later). In her house she had set up an oratory where the Blessed Sacrament was reserved. Anxious to make me feel at home and to make the transition from convent life as smooth as possible, she had equipped the bathroom of the apartment with every conceivable cosmetic and packed the fridge with food. She was pressing in her invitations to join her for a meal, sit with her in the garden, watch television with her ... and I couldn't bear any of it. I didn't want sympathy, I didn't want concern, I didn't want human company. All I wanted was to be somewhere quiet where I could curl up and lick my wounds and try to come to terms with what had happened. I must have been a most unpleasant tenant.

On the third day, just when I was wondering whether I could tolerate another minute of life in Metz, an escape route offered itself. My friend Tom Cranfield, then deputy registrar at the European Court of Justice in Luxembourg, rang to say that a firm of English lawyers in Luxembourg were looking for an English-speaking lawyer. In my anxiety to clutch at any straw, I was convinced that this was the answer to all my prayers. I had no doubt whatsoever that I would get the job. By five o'clock that evening I had phoned the law firm, faxed them my CV, had a response inviting me to an interview the following day, booked a room in the Hotel Schintgen on the rue Notre Dame for a week and told Mlle Martin that I was moving to Luxembourg after all. She was very good about it and even allowed me to leave a lot of my belongings behind, on the understanding that I would come and reclaim them when I had somewhere to live. That night, overwhelmed with relief, I had my first proper night's sleep since leaving Chambarand.

Early next morning, I said goodbye to Mlle Martin, collected my luggage and took the bus into the centre of Metz. My train wasn't until midday, but I wanted to go shopping: I had nothing suitable to wear for an interview. In Printemps, I bought a tailored black jacket and trousers and a white shirt – lawyer dress. I was heading back into a familiar life again, and this was the first step.

On the train to Luxembourg, I was euphoric. Everything was going to be all right. In no time at all I would be back where I belonged and all the unhappy events of the past year and a half would be as if they had never happened. Of course, there wasn't much hope that I could recover my old apartment; that had surely been leased to someone else, but perhaps I could find one in the same neighbourhood. I imagined myself sitting once again on a balcony in the late evening, looking across at the distant hill, sipping wine and listening to Paul Simon. I must ask my sister for that CD back, I thought, a warm feeling of anticipation stealing over me. I leaned back in my seat and watched the familiar stations flying past: Bridel, Dommeldange … I was at home again. I looked back in amazement at the state I had been in for the past few weeks, and especially since coming to Metz. It was clear to me now that all I had needed was to get back to somewhere I knew and where I had been happy. I felt absolutely fine.

Outside the railway station in Luxembourg I waited for a bus to bring me into Place Hamilius. How good it was to know exactly where I was going and how to get there! The Hotel Schintgen was familiar too: I had stayed there for a while when I had first come to Luxembourg. Bathed in the bliss that follows the relief from pain, I unpacked my bags, showered, donned the black suit and surveyed myself in the long mirror on the back of the wardrobe door. Yes, I looked fine. Hair still a bit too short, perhaps, but it was growing every day. A quick spray of Miss Dior and I was ready to go.

Five minutes into the interview at the law firm's offices, my euphoria had vanished and I knew I had made a big mistake. They were looking for a tax expert, and they had the wrong person: tax law was something I had always avoided like the plague. I wondered why they had bothered to interview me, as it was clear from my CV that tax was not one of my areas. I wasn't left wondering very long. When I explained that I didn't 'do' tax, the balding forty-ish lawyer who was interviewing me said,

'Oh yes, I realised that. But I was curious about this recent entry on your CV. You were in a convent for the past two years?'

So that was it: I was there simply to gratify his curiosity. Squirming with embarrassment and bitterly disappointed, I answered his few perfunctory questions and got myself out of there somehow. Back in my room in the Hotel Schintgen, I looked bleakly down on the busy street below. 'The mind is its own place,' said Milton truly, 'and in itself can make a heaven of hell, a hell of heaven.' Luxembourg was the same place it had been three hours earlier, when arriving there had felt like a triumphant homecoming. Now I realised that it, too, was built at the edge of that awful void. Only now did I realise how heavily I had relied on the prospect of getting a job again in Luxembourg. I hadn't thought beyond that; I had no other plans, no idea what

I was going to do. I couldn't stay in Luxembourg indefinitely. I had a small sum of money which I had brought with me to contribute to the community when I entered Aubépine, and which the nuns had returned to me when I left. It was all I had to live on until I could get a job, but it would not last very long if I spent too much time in hotels. And I flatly refused to even consider returning to Metz.

In this way began the most desolate period I had experienced since leaving Aubépine. It was to a large extent my own fault. I had plenty of friends in Luxembourg, but with one or two exceptions, they didn't yet know that I had left Aubépine. I didn't feel ready to meet anyone at the moment, and so I hadn't even told Tom Cranfield that I had arranged an interview with the law firm he had so kindly told me about. He didn't know I was in Luxembourg. The only person who knew I was there was Valérie Saintot, a friend and former colleague from the Court of Justice. I had phoned her before I left Metz, and we had arranged to meet for dinner on the evening of my interview. I had expected to be celebrating my new job and had been very upbeat on the phone, so it had been a great shock to poor Valérie to find me on the edge of tears throughout the meal. Another day, crossing the bridge over the Petrousse Valley, I bumped into Mafalda Rizzolati, another former colleague. Astonished and delighted to see me, she stopped, full of questions, and was very distressed when I burst into tears there on the street. So really, I felt it was better to avoid old friends.

A day or two after the interview I was wandering aimlessly about the city, panic threatening to invade me at every moment, when, around three o'clock, I found myself in the rue des Capucins, near the church of St Alphonse. This was the church where I used to attend Mass every evening on my way home from the court. There was an Irish priest, Father Patrick O'Connor, attached to the church. I didn't know him very well, but suddenly I wanted desperately to talk to somebody Irish. I walked around the corner to the door of the monastery attached to the church, hoping he would be there. He was. He came running down the stairs and stopped dead when he saw me, a look of astonishment on his face. The last time he had seen me was when I had called to say goodbye a year and a half earlier.

'What on earth …' he began.

At the sound of the familiar Irish accent I did my by now usual trick of bursting into tears. Appalled, the poor man ushered me anxiously into a small parlour, and fussed around for a few minutes organising cups of tea, the Irish panacea for all ills. Taking a gulp of hot tea and a few deep breaths, I tried to calm down and explain what had happened. The incoherent story couldn't have made much sense to him, but he made comforting and reassuring noises and poured out another cup of tea. He insisted that I should come back and have dinner with him at seven that evening.

'We can think a bit then about what you should do next,' he said encouragingly.

This gave me a focus for the rest of the day. I decided I would go to Mass in St Alphonse at six o'clock, and meet Fr O'Connor afterwards.

So it was in a slightly more positive frame of mind that I left the monastery and headed back up the rue des Capucins to the Place d'Armes. In spite of the lateness of the season, Luxembourg was hanging on to summer and the square was colourful with the red and yellow umbrellas on the tables outside the restaurants. A band was playing martial airs in the bandstand and a busker with a red plastic nose was entertaining al-fresco diners by the simple expedient of following passers-by and imitating, unknown to them, their gait and gestures. He was the same busker whose antics had reduced my sister and me to hysterical laughter a few summers earlier during a visit she had made to Luxembourg. Memories of this happier time threatening to overcome me once again, I shut them out and hurried on through the square. Near the Pizza Hut was a small newsagent and tobacconist and as I passed it, I remembered that it was one of the few places in Luxembourg where the *Irish Times* was sold. Realising that I could read the *Irish Times* for the first time in almost two years, I went in. I was in luck; it had arrived that day. I bought it, went out again to the square, sat down at a seat near the fountain and opened the paper with a sudden rush of anticipation to find out what was happening in Ireland.

The front page had a large photograph of someone I recognised from my old days in the law: Professor Mary McAleese, the head of the Institute of Professional Legal Studies in Belfast. Astonished, I read that she was running for election as the next President of Ireland. Well, my goodness! Elsewhere on the same page I learned that the Taoiseach had ordered an internal inquiry into apparent corruption in the urban planning process. It seemed that bribes might have been offered and accepted, and planning permission granted where it should have been refused. The Taoiseach would decide later, I read, what further action to take, although he ruled out referring the controversy to the new Moriarty Tribunal. Moriarty Tribunal? What on earth was that? I realised I would need an intensive course in Irish politics and news in order to catch up. It was a strange, Rip Van Winkle-ish feeling.

There was a lot I didn't know. For example, I didn't know that another tribunal – the McCracken Tribunal – had only a few weeks earlier published a report in which it revealed the existence of secret accounts held in the Cayman Islands by prominent Irish business people and politicians. Two years later, that report was to affect my life in a totally unforeseeable way.

As I was about to turn over the page, my eye was caught by a small notice at the top. 'Careers,' it said. '18 pages of jobs. The *Irish Times* has all the best moves.' Of course. It was Friday; the day the paper published all the job ads. Well, I might as well start looking. Without much hope, I turned to the business section. Flicking through it, my eye was caught by the heading 'Legal Adviser'. I read on. The Irish Competition Authority was looking for a barrister to act as legal adviser. The closing date for applications was some three weeks ahead. Application forms were available from the Civil Service Commission. I got up, went straight to the post office on the Place Hamilius, phoned the number given in the ad and asked them to send an application form to my friend Sheelagh O'Driscoll's address in Cork. Then I phoned Sheelagh, told her what I had done, and said that I would check with her in a few days' time to see whether it had arrived. Feeling, if not exactly hopeful, at least a little encouraged that I had taken some sort of step about my future, I went back to the Hotel Schintgen.

Later, I returned to the Place d'Armes to meet Fr O'Connor. We went to the Pizza Hut and sat at a table outside in the balmy evening. I couldn't eat. My appetite, which had been good in Chambarand, had disappeared in Metz and hadn't returned. There was a hard lump lodged in my chest which seemed to prevent the swallowing of any food. To my embarrassment, Fr O'Connor insisted on paying for my uneaten pizza. He had been thinking hard in the few hours that had intervened since our previous meeting, and now he wanted to give me the fruit of his meditations. He was convinced I should go back to Ireland. I told him about the *Irish Times* ad, and he was pleased that I had shown some initiative, but urged me not to wait to see whether anything came of it.

'You really would feel so much better at home,' he said. 'Apart from anything else, you would be in a better position to find out what jobs were available.'

I knew he was right, yet I couldn't make up my mind to leave Luxembourg. In some vague and irrational way, I felt that if I left Luxembourg I would be breaking my final link with Aubépine and would be at last admitting that there was no going back.

Among the miserable and desolate days that followed, one stands out. In search of some way of filling in the empty hours, I went to the bus station and took the bus to Echternach, a small town about forty miles away where I used to like to spend the occasional day in pre-Aubépine times. Echternach is a pretty town that attracts many tourists, and I had always enjoyed the bus journey through the Luxembourg countryside. But that day, nothing brought me peace. Filled with inner agitation, I got out of the bus in Echternach, walked to the end of the street, went to a coffee-shop, had a coffee and got the next bus back to Luxembourg. All afternoon, I wandered hopelessly around the city, unable to relax anywhere, weak tears constantly starting to my eyes. At six o'clock I went as usual to St Alphonse for Mass, but I might as well have been out in the street for all that I was aware of what was going on. I couldn't concentrate. Throughout Mass, I kept fighting tears. Finally, I felt I would have to leave. At that moment, I realised that all around me people were getting up to go to communion. Hardly knowing what I was doing, I stood up and followed them, wiping away tears as I stumbled towards the altar. The priest gave me the host, and I placed it in my mouth, intending to walk directly to the door and leave. I was so distracted by my own pain that I was hardly aware that I had received communion. And then, without warning, as I turned away from the altar a total stillness fell upon me. I felt utterly at peace. My tears had dried up as though they had never existed. I returned to my seat and sat down, relishing the bliss of freedom from pain. I stayed there for a long time before finally going out to find a restaurant for dinner. My appetite had returned; I was filled with a sense of well-being. I ate a hearty meal, and that night I slept without dreams. Some sort of turning-point had been reached, some sort of inner reassurance had been given and received. On a conscious level, I still had no idea what to do, but at that deep level that I had come to know in Aubépine, that level where God is active, some secret core of me knew that all was not irretrievably lost. If I had been capable during those days of reading my old friend John of the Cross, I might have discovered what was happening and been reassured.

> There are intervals of relief in the process of purification (he says in the *Dark Night*) during which, by God's grace, contemplation ceases to be dark and oppressive and instead is felt as loving and full of light. Then the soul is like someone who has been released from prison. It feels a sense of space and liberation, of peace and of the close friendship of God.

I was, then, in a better frame of mind than at any other time since

I had left Aubépine, when something happened that was to put an end to all this aimless wandering around France and Luxembourg. The evening before I left Aubépine, the nuns had given me a present. At recreation, Véronique had handed me a large gift-wrapped box.

'We thought that this would be something you would like,' she had said, smiling rather anxiously.

I had stood there, not wanting to open it. I didn't want presents. I just wanted them to change their minds and let me stay.

'Go on,' Véronique had urged, 'open it!'

I had opened it awkwardly: it was a portable CD player, with two small loudspeakers. At the time, I had been overcome by a mixture of emotions: I was touched by the gift, which showed how well the nuns knew me, and at the same time I was resentful of the fact that they thought it could make any difference in the larger scheme of things. I probably hadn't shown enough gratitude and indeed, I packed it away and didn't really feel like looking at it again for quite some time. But I was now feeling so much more myself that I wanted to listen to some music, so the day after the experience in St Alphonse I unpacked the CD player from its box and set it up in my hotel room. I had brought some CDs with me when I joined the community at Aubépine, and the nuns had returned them to me when I was leaving. Rooting through them now, I found one with a collection of sacred music and, plugging in the earphones, I put it on. With huge pleasure, I was listening to Robert Gambill singing the *Cujus Animam* from Rossini's *Stabat Mater* when I realised that some other noise was going on in the room. I pulled out the earphones: it was the telephone ringing.

I had by this time contacted a few friends in Ireland to give them the news. Each conversation made me feel just a little bit better, and most of my friends took the phone number of my hotel so that they could keep in touch. I picked up the phone.

'Noreenyboots! Is it really you?' I knew that cheerful and friendly voice immediately. Besides, there was only one person in the world who called me by that ridiculous name.

'Bart!' I exclaimed in disbelief, and then, as usual, burst into tears.

Bart Daly was a legal publisher. When I had first got to know him in my early days at the Bar, he had been editor of the *Irish Law Reports Monthly* at Round Hall Press. In those days, he had come to my rescue, as he had come to the rescue of many another young and impoverished barrister, by commissioning me to write law reports for his publication. This activity became my principal means of subsistence during the thin days of my early legal practice. Meanwhile, Bart and his wife Stephanie became my enduring friends.

Now here he was on the telephone, shaken by my reaction and trying, with the helplessness such things induce when you are thousands of miles away, to comfort me.

'Noreen,' he said, 'you should come home to where your friends are. I can give you enough freelance work to keep you busy for a couple of months. I need a proof-reader. I need some-one to research stuff for a book. I could really do with you.'

I didn't believe a word of it. Bart is one of the kindest people I know, and I suspected that he would invent work, if necessary, in order to help me. But it was, oh, so comforting! He explained that he was no longer with Round Hall, but had set up on his own, and that this was why he was in a position to employ me. Suddenly, Dublin seemed infinitely attractive. I decided to go home.

CHAPTER FOUR

O woods and thickets,
planted by the hand of the Beloved!
O meadows of verdure, enamelled with flowers,
Say if he has passed by you.

The plane taxied down the runway at Cork airport. It was Thursday the second of October 1997 and I was returning to Ireland after an absence of over four years. I disembarked, and within a short time I was greeting Sheelagh O'Driscoll at the meeting point in the arrivals lounge. I smiled and hugged her, but she was not fooled. My desolation could not be hidden. I felt very strange, as though my body had arrived a split second ahead of my spirit, and would not wait to let it catch up. I could feel my spirit running along behind me, giving little breathless gasps. My legs marched along, but inside me was a hole through which the air was pouring out. We went to Sheelagh's house, which I had never seen before – she had bought it in my absence. Later, her fiancé, Matthew arrived; he was new to me too. What a lot had happened while I was away!

My plan was to stay with Sheelagh for a few days, and then to go to Dublin to look for somewhere to live. Somehow, I hadn't been able to face arriving straight into Dublin, with all that it implied of being greeted by family and friends. Sheelagh's house on Gardiner's Hill was a haven of peace and she just let me get on with things at my own pace. The area she was living in was familiar too, and that helped. My aunt and uncle had lived all their lives just around the corner on Old Youghal Road, and I had spent many summer holidays there as a child. In more recent years I had visited my uncle Willie as often as possible, as he struggled with old age, failing health, and the loneliness in which he had lived since the death of Mina, his sister. Now they were both gone and the house had been sold. The morning after my arrival, when Sheelagh had left to go to her office, I walked around the corner and stood in front of it. The door and windows had been replaced and the pocket-sized front garden tidied up. The decrepit, falling-to-bits house of the last few years was now looking quite smart: a desirably trendy town house. Somehow, though, it had lost something. I wondered what the back garden looked like now. In my childhood, it was a magical place. You walked through the back door of the house into a sunny white-washed yard where, facing you, a short flight of steps led through an opening in the wall to the garden proper. There the grass was always allowed to grow a little in the summer, unlike the shaved and manicured lawn favoured by my father in our own house. In Mina and Willie's house, there were always daisies and buttercups available for making daisy-chains, and a small child could lie on her back and watch the butterflies weaving in and out of the tall blades of grass over her head. It was a garden for dreaming in.

Indeed, the whole of Cork had a dream-like quality to it in my childhood. It was a place that existed only in the summer holidays. I knew Mina and Willie lived somewhere during the rest of the year, but I couldn't believe it was the same place. That place was a summer place; it was impossible to imagine it with leafless trees or frosty grass. It was a special place: in Cork, even the van that delivered the bread had a different sound. It spoke with a Cork accent, the sound of its engine rising as it climbed the hill towards my aunt's house. As I lay in bed on those delicious holiday mornings, the sound of the bread van's engine was as evocative of summer as the cooing of the wood pigeons in the garden outside the bedroom window.

In Cork in those days, everything was different from the way it was at home. Milk, for example, was not delivered prosaically in bottles to the doorstep. It appeared inside the house, as if by magic. Mina would leave the empty white blue-rimmed milk-jug with its little muslin bonnet on the inside sill of the front window. The milkman, when he came in his horse-drawn van full of churns, would lift up the lower part of the sash window, fill the jug, put its little bonnet back on, replace it on the window-sill and close the window again.

For all of these reasons, it had been a good decision to come first to Cork. It allowed me time to realise that I was back in Ireland while at the same time giving me a breathing-space before real life began at last.

Because indeed I knew now that I had to face a future that was not in Aubépine. The period of denial was over: I no longer expected a phone-call from Véronique or Marie-Jeanne telling me that they had made a terrible mistake, and asking me to come back, although my conviction that they had indeed been mistaken still endured. There were a number of things I had to do. First, I had to fill out the application form for the job in the Competition Authority, which I had found waiting for me in Sheelagh's house when I arrived. Next, I had to find somewhere to live in Dublin, so that I could take up Bart Daly's offer and begin the research he wanted me to do. Finally, I had to keep looking for a job, because I knew there was no great likelihood that I would succeed in getting the one in the Competition Authority.

So that Friday, after I had returned from my nostalgic visit to the house of my aunt and uncle, I sat down in Sheelagh's book-lined livingroom-cum-kitchen and filled out the Competition Authority application form. Then I telephoned a B&B in Dublin and booked myself in from Saturday evening until Tuesday. I hoped that a long weekend would be enough time to get some sort of temporary accommodation. Later that evening I met Sheelagh for dinner in Isaacs' restaurant, and told her what I had planned. We arranged that I would come back to Cork on Tuesday, either to collect my belongings or to trespass on her hospitality for another few days, depending on whether I had found somewhere to live or not.

Three days later I sat drinking coffee with Kay Clancy in the Tara Towers Hotel on Merrion Road in Dublin, waiting for it to be two o'clock. I had viewed a small one-bedroom flat on the top floor of a red-brick terraced house in Ballsbridge and I had told the agent I wanted to take it. It was a far cry from my old, spacious Luxembourg apartment, and it had no balcony, but the rent was within my means and the window of its tiny living room looked out over the rooftops of Ballsbridge. The only problem was that I was not the only person interested in it. I had been obliged to join a queue to view it at eleven o' clock that morning, and I was one of at least three people who had said they wanted to take it. The estate agent who had been showing the flat had told us all to phone at two o'clock, by which time, in some mysterious way, a decision would have been made.

So it was that I was now sitting, heart in mouth, watching the hands of the clock in the Tara Towers slowly approach the fatal hour. As soon as I had left the flat, I had phoned Kay, and she had immediately driven over from Portmarnock to keep vigil with me.

Kay and I went back a long way. We were nine years old when we first met. I had just started a new school, and was badly missing my old friends. Kay was in my new class, but I didn't really became aware of her until a few weeks later, at a school film, where we happened to be sitting side by side.

'I can see the film in your glasses,' she announced after the first five minutes, peering into my face.

Ever since, whenever I hear the plaintive strains of *Róisín Dubh*, the theme music from that film, I see hovering in front of me Kay's pale nine-year old face with its sprinkling of freckles and its two prominent front teeth, eyes squinting in an attempt to follow the action reflected in my plastic-rimmed glasses. It was the beginning of a friendship that lasted through primary and secondary school, surviving my first teenage attempt at religious life and her own marriage. Kay was always there, closer than a sister, an extension of myself.

And so it was that she now stood anxiously behind me as I phoned the estate agent from a public telephone in the Tara Towers and learned that – by what process of elimination of the other contenders I do not know – I had got the flat. I had a home again. Another missing part clicked into place inside me.

CHAPTER FIVE

Scattering a thousand graces,
He passed through these woods in haste,
And looking upon them as he went,
Left them, by his glance alone, clothed with beauty.

One Monday morning in early November I locked the door of the flat behind me and set off along Merrion Road. I was on my way to the library in Kings Inns, to continue the research I had begun for Bart. It was four weeks since I had moved into my new flat, and I had acquired a daily routine. It was almost – but not quite – like being a member of the workforce again. It was just that I wasn't too sure of my identity. If someone had stopped me on the street as I made my way to the number 7 bus-stop and had asked me 'what do you do for a living?' I wouldn't have known how to answer. In the past, I now realised, I had never answered that question literally, by saying, for example, 'I practise law.' I had always replied in a way that defined my identity: I am a barrister, I am a Carmelite. Now for the first time it struck me as odd that I had always thought of myself in terms of what I did rather than of who I was. So who was I, and why did I feel not fully complete if I couldn't define myself by an oc-cupation? The truth was, I realised, that as I walked down Merrion Road that morning, I felt somehow less of a person than all the other commuters who were getting into their cars and waiting at bus-stops, in spite of the fact that I was carrying a briefcase and would be paid for the work that I was about to do. I realised my image of myself needed some work. I believed – and would have said, if asked – that I was a person loved by God, and that it was this which gave meaning to my life. Nevertheless, that intellectual conviction did not seem to have reached my gut.

This may have been connected, to some degree, with my prayer-life, which seemed to me to be practically dead. Since I arrived home, I had tried to sort out in my mind what I was supposed to do in the spiritual field. For the previous four years, I had believed that I had a vocation to live as a contemplative, to make the quest of union with God the sole purpose of my life. I had thought that the only way in which I could fully respond to this vocation was by joining a contemplative community, where I would have nothing else to do but contemplate, where even the work I did would be conducive to inner quiet.

Now, I was back in the world of law. How could I be a contemplative? Was I mistaken in believing that it was my vocation? That, of course, was the one question I was still avoiding. If I had to face the fact that it was all an illusion, the tenuous scaffolding on which I was trying to rebuild my shattered life would collapse. Prayer still seduced me: the word 'God', appearing in the most mundane context, never failed to light some sort of inner firework, so that the word seemed to leap out surrounded by flames from a page, or explode from the radio or from a conversation with fanfares of trumpets. And yet, I couldn't pray.

I thought discipline might be the way. So I established a rule of life for myself, dividing the day up between work and prayer almost as if I were back in the convent. But all that this ploy seemed to produce was stress. In order to have time both to pray and to attend Mass before starting the daily routine in Kings Inns, I got up at about five-thirty, spent an hour in a futile and increasingly frustrating attempt to pray, had breakfast and set off to get the bus into town where I went to Mass in Clarendon Street en route to Kings Inns. But the hour of prayer simply wasn't working. Gone were the magical early mornings of Aubépine, where that first hour of the day in the darkened chapel brought me to a still and secret place. Instead, I came out of my tiny bedroom (only just big enough to hold the bed), into my equally tiny livingroom-cum-kitchen, where I sat on the floor in the corner facing the door (the emptiest corner of the cluttered space) and tried to find the lost secret garden. Nothing worked. Instead of the secret garden I seemed to enter a place of demons. That silent inner space where in the past I had found

God, or so I believed, was now filed with raucous voices which called everything, including God himself, into question. Other angry and bitter voices rehearsed over and over again every misunderstanding that had ever occurred between me and Marie-Jeanne, the novice mistress in Aubépine. I sat there as my thoughts whirled and my frustration level rose to screaming pitch.

Thinking a retreat might help, I booked into a retreat house run by Carmelite friars in Donnybrook, not far from where I was living. It was a disaster. I couldn't concentrate on the talks that were given, I couldn't pray. I spent the entire time wishing the clock around and it was with great relief that I left at the end of the five prescribed days.

Early in December, I had a welcome break from all of this when I went back to Metz to collect the belongings I had left in Mlle Martin's house. Valérie Saintot had arranged to come with me to help me transfer the stuff. So, armed with three empty suitcases, I went first to Luxembourg where I stayed the night in Valérie's flat. Our dinner that evening was more successful than the one we had a few months earlier, and Valérie was relieved to find a Noreen who was more like her old self. We drove to Metz, where Mlle Martin entertained us to lunch and I was able at last to thank her properly for her hospitality. Returning to Dublin with suitcases packed full of sheets and towels, I felt that a chapter had been closed.

But back home again, prayer continued to be a major problem. By the end of December I was desperate. I needed an adviser, but where could I turn? I didn't know anyone in Dublin to whom I could talk about such things. One day, I suddenly thought: I know what I need to do, I need to talk to a Jesuit. To this day, I'm not sure why exactly this thought came to me. I knew no Jesuits. It may have been a combination of the fact that the only community retreat I had attended in Aubépine had been given by a Jesuit who had deeply impressed me and the fact that Teresa of Avila, whose autobiography I was re-reading, had been sorted out herself by a Jesuit at a time when her own spiritual life was in deep confusion. Anyway, whatever the

41

motivation, I thumbed through the telephone directory on the first Friday of January 1998, and found a phone number for a Jesuit house in Dollymount, just beyond Clontarf on the North Dublin coast. The friendly woman who answered the phone seemed a little puzzled by my request to see a priest – any priest – but she went off to enquire and in due course returned to say that if I would call over at two o'clock the next afternoon, I would be able to see somebody.

On the next afternoon, filled with anticipation, I boarded the number 130 bus in Lower Abbey Street. The bus journey to Dollymount is a pleasant one. Just past Fairview, the sea comes into view, and from there on the road hugs the coastline. Shortly afterwards, the bus passes the little village of Clontarf on the left, its period redbrick seafront houses familiar to me from childhood days at the seaside. Dollymount was where we usually went on day-trips. After Clontarf, faces glued to the window of the bus, we would watch for the first sight of the wooden bridge at the Bull Wall, that long bridge leading out to the sea – a pier, really – which we had to march along until we came to the lovely sandy beach. Thrillingly, you could see the sea between the wooden planks of the bridge where they didn't quite meet, and there was always in my mind the excitingly frightening possibility that we might fall through and be drowned. It lent a certain *frisson* to our summer outings.

Little had changed along the route in the years that had passed since those childhood days. True, there were new apartment blocks here and there, but somehow they merged into the general residential appearance of the place, so that the road still looked the same. There was only one change that jarred. Opposite the Bull Wall there had been in my childhood a row of houses that I had looked forward to seeing on each trip. They had a seaside character that was totally lacking in ordinary inland houses such as the one we lived in ourselves: they had a little circular window beside the hall door. I had only ever seen such a thing on pictures of ships in books, and I was quite sure that you could only have a porthole in your house if you lived beside the sea. Now, as the bus passed the Bull Wall, I looked in vain for the porthole houses, but they had gone. Newer houses with ordinary windows had taken their place.

Manresa House, the Jesuit retreat and conference centre in Dollymount, is built, strangely, with its back to the sea. It has had a varied history. Originally named Baymount House, it was at one time the home of Dr Trail, Protestant Bishop of Down and Connor. Subsequently, it was in turn a school run by the Loreto sisters and a private junior school known as Baymount Castle Preparatory School. The Jesuits have been there for many years, and at one time their noviciate was there. Now it is a centre of spirituality where they run retreats, courses and workshops.

I got off the bus at the gate, and made my way up the long tree-lined driveway, where in spring and summer one runs a gauntlet of generous bird-droppings. For Manresa, with its profuse and varied trees and its proximity to the nearby bird sanctuary at Bull Island, is a paradise for birds of every description. Each year during their regular visit to the Irish coast, flocks of Brent geese land at evening on the lawn while the shadows of the trees lengthen slowly across it.

About half-way up the drive, the house itself comes into view, the original building concealed from that side by the modern buildings of the retreat house. Not knowing where exactly to go, I made my way past the retreat house and followed the drive as it swept around to face the little castle itself. An elderly man admitted me, and I was led into a formal reception room with the shiny overstuffed straight-backed chairs that are such a feature of religious institutions in Ireland. I felt nervous. I didn't know where to begin my story, or how to make this unknown Jesuit understand what had happened. While I was still trying to plan my speech, the door opened and Father Finbarr Lynch and his Cork accent walked into my life. Somehow, once I began to talk to this rather studious-looking, silver-haired man, there was no difficulty. I felt totally at ease, and he seemed to understand straight away what my problem was. Once I had finished my story, he got briskly to the point.

'An eight-day directed retreat just began here yesterday,' he said, 'Why not join in?'

'Oh, I couldn't,' I said, suddenly panic-stricken, remembering the disastrous retreat in November. 'I have a family commitment next Wednesday evening ...'

'Well,' said Finbarr mildly, 'you could come tomorrow morning and leave on Wednesday morning. Today is Saturday. That would give you three full days and a bit at each end.'

'But I couldn't possibly begin tomorrow,' I interjected, appalled. 'I have lots of things to do. I have to ...'

My voice tailed off. What, in fact, had I to do? Nothing.

'Well, all right,' I said, defeated. 'I'll come tomorrow.'

Finbarr dropped me back into town that Saturday afternoon, and left me in Marlboro Street. I went into Easons, hardly knowing what I was doing. Flicking unseeing through the latest arrivals, I mentally chastised myself for my inability to say no. Why on earth had I agreed to lock myself up for the next few days? Was I completely mad? Finbarr had told me what the retreat would be like. I would see him for a half an hour each day, and for the rest I would be left to my own devices, in total silence. There would be a Mass each evening at which all the retreatants would participate, but there would be no other exercises in common. Meals, although taken together, would be taken in silence. I wasn't able at the moment to spend even ten minutes in prayer; faced with this terrible programme, how would I cope?

So it was that, filled with foreboding, I left the flat before eight o'clock the following morning and headed out into the empty Sunday street, carrying a bag with a couple of changes of clothes and as many books as I could fit into it. I had agonised over the choice of books the previous night. It was clear to me that I would need to bring as many as possible, so as to fill in the empty hours that stretched ahead. Accordingly, I had brought the *Complete Works of St John of the Cross* (four volumes), a book in French called *Le Combat de Jacob*, which had helped me greatly in Aubépine and Thomas Merton's *Seven Storey Mountain*. Six books. I hoped it would be enough: there were a lot of hours to fill in. Still, the Merton was a sizable volume: it should be good for at least one day. Looking at it, I had felt a bit more cheerful. With enough books, I could survive anything.

The weather was dry and bright and not too cold; good retreat weather, Finbarr said when he met me at the door of the retreat house. He picked up a key from the hall table, and brought me upstairs to my room. It was a small room. (Another small room: all the rooms I had inhabited since leaving Luxembourg two years previously had been small. I seemed to move in a Lilliputian world.) The first thing that struck me about it was the sense of peace that hung over it; in it I felt I was breathing the same air that had filled my cell in Aubépine. There is no doubt that a place that is prayed in has a particular quality; the air in it is dense with the breath of God. It is when coming into one of these special places that are like half-open doors between heaven and this world that we realise that the kingdom of heaven is here and now. Jacob knew it when he woke after his dream of angels climbing a ladder from the place where he was lying into heaven, and back again. Overcome with awe, he exclaimed,

> How awesome is this place. This is none other than the house of God, and this is the gate of heaven.

Poets have always known it too:

> O world invisible, we view thee,
> O world intangible, we touch thee,
> O world unknowable, we know thee,
> Inapprehensible, we clutch thee!

said Francis Thompson, who, in his turn, saw the same ladder fixed between heaven and Charing Cross.

This particular ante-room of heaven had brick walls painted white, a single bed, a small wardrobe, a wash basin, and a window overlooking the garden. On the wall hung a large colour photograph, mounted and framed. It showed a forest path leading through woods into the distance, and underneath was written a verse from psalm 83: 'They are happy whose strength is in you, in whose hearts are the roads to Sion.' I thought of the French translation, which is particularly beautiful, and as I looked at that picture so full of mystery and of tranquillity I repeated it to myself: *des chemins s'ouvrent dans leur coeur*: They are happy whose strength is in you; paths open in their hearts. I had always preferred this translation, indicating as it did the opening of ways where none had previously existed. During my most difficult times in Aubépine, when I could not see any way forward, I repeated that phrase over and over, hoping that someday a path would open in my own heart.

I unpacked my few items of clothing and my large number of books, and went back downstairs to have my first retreat meeting with Finbarr ('a chat' was how he always described these occasions). This particular chat was to introduce me to the retreat, and to suggest a passage of scripture that I might meditate on for the day. I made my way through the entrance hall and along the corridor that led to the diningroom, turning left as instructed at St Ignatius' Corridor. Finbarr's room was number 11, the second on the right. It was a room that was to become very familiar to me over the following years.

Inside, it was unexpectedly cosy and comfortable. There were armchairs and soft lamps, and on the low table at my elbow I noticed a box of tissues. Was he expecting me to cry, then? Were the tissues always there, or were they just for me? I didn't know. It was all a bit strange. I had never had a spiritual director before. Our conversation began. I mentioned the books I had brought. Finbarr was amused.

'Well,' he said, 'I don't really think you'll need them. I usually discourage books during retreat, as it's essential to get rid of all the inner noise and clutter that you'll have brought with you. Reading will only add to it.'

I was alarmed and not a little shocked. John of the Cross add to 'clutter'? Surely not! Much later I understood what Finbarr meant. Times of retreat are principally times of listening. A great inner silence is necessary for this, and it can take days to achieve anything approximating it. Nowadays I wouldn't dream of bringing books with me on retreat, knowing that my time will be fully occupied with inner events, with prayer and with discernment.

But, 'I don't think I could manage without the books,' I told Finbarr now.

'Well, I won't force you,' he said. 'Let's see how you get on.' And with that I had to be content.

So the first day of the retreat began: a retreat that was to change everything.

CHAPTER SIX

Ah, who will be able to heal me?
Surrender thou thyself now completely.
From today do thou send me now no other messengers
For they cannot tell me what I wish.

The previous day hadn't been an easy one, as I explained to Finbarr, discouraged, when we met for our 'chat' the following morning. Prayer was just as difficult as ever – indeed, if anything, it was more difficult, because there was so much of it. Finbarr had suggested that I spend four hours in prayer each day, interspersed with reading the scripture passage he had given me and some walks. I had followed this programme as best as I could, but, as always, whenever I tried to settle down to pray my mind would fill with images of Aubépine, of Véronique and of Marie-Jeanne. Despite my best efforts, I found myself replaying those final days, and all the associated emotions of loss and anger surged up again inside me and threatened to suffocate me. How could I pray?

Finbarr looked thoughtfully at me as I listed my woes.

'I don't think you've grieved properly yet for what you've lost', he said. 'You need to really feel the loss. Why don't you try praying in your room today instead of in the chapel, and when you start to feel anger or pain or sadness or whatever, let it come. You'll probably cry a lot, but that will be good, and as there won't be anyone there to see you, you won't be embarrassed.'

To be honest, this was not what I wanted to hear. I wanted to transcend all these feelings that were getting the better of me and my prayer, not to submerge myself in them in what sounded to me like a very self-indulgent manner. I opened my mouth to argue, and then shut it again. I was beginning to realise how little I really knew and a faint suspicion was starting to form that the less noble my deeds were, the more authentic they were likely to be. What was more, I already trusted Finbarr. So I swallowed my objections, went to my room and tried to pray. And all happened exactly as he had predicted. Overwhelmed by the realisation that I had lost Aubépine, the community, Véronique and Marie-Jeanne, that I had lost too all that it implied of a life wholly given to prayer and contemplation, and acknowledging fully to myself for the first time that there was no going back, I wept bitterly. And that evening, when I had no more tears left, I sat up, blew my nose, looked around me and saw that I was free. 'My harness piece by piece Thou hast hewn from me,' said Francis Thompson, describing a similar experience. Thinking of him, I remembered other lines from the same poem:

All which I took from thee I did but take,
Not for thy harms,
But just that thou might'st seek it in My arms.
All which thy child's mistake
Fancies as lost, I have stored for thee at home:
Rise, clasp My hand, and come!

Was this what was happening? Had Aubépine been taken from me so that I might look for what I was seeking in God? A first, faint glimmer of understanding began to dawn on me.

At our meeting the following day, Finbarr was very pleased with what I had to report. He said:

'Now you must learn to trust your prayer. It may seem messy and distracted, and indeed may not seem to be prayer at all, but believe me, it is good. Trust it, go with it. After all, when you pray, you are not the only person involved. Do you think God does nothing during prayer? Trust him now; let go, and see what he will do.'

I wasn't too sure what he meant. I explained again that simply nothing was happening during prayer.

'And how do you know that?' he enquired.

'Well, because I get distracted.'

'When you say "distracted", do you mean that you get bored, and start to pursue a more interesting line of thought?'

I didn't have to give this too much thought.

49

'Oh, no. No, it's more that all sorts of half-baked thoughts and images keep floating in and out of my mind, so that I can't hold on to the idea of God, or the awareness that I'm there with him, or ...'

'Look', said Finbarr, patiently, 'the fact is that you are there with him, whether you feel it or not. You don't have to be aware of it to make it true. As I keep telling you, it's not *your* prayer; it's *our* prayer – yours and God's. Someone else besides you is involved.'

'Think of it like this,' he went on. 'Imagine a mother with small, noisy children. One day, a friend comes to visit her. She really wants to have a good chat with this friend, so she sends the children off to play upstairs. However, they're not so far away that she can't still hear them. The noise they are making could be distracting, certainly. So this woman can do one of two things: she can keep running upstairs to try to quieten them down, probably without much of a result. And each time she does this, she has to leave her friend. Or she can decide to let the noise go on and just ignore it. After some time, it will simply become background noise. There are two important things to notice about the second option: one, she doesn't leave her friend at all, and two, the noise won't stop! Now go away and just try it out. Remember that God wants to meet you during this time of prayer. He may have things to say to you. It may be that all you're required to do is simply show up and stay there for the allotted time.'

A bit dubiously, I went off to try it out. I don't think I could even have made the attempt a few days earlier, but the lifting of the anguish and bitterness over Aubépine had already begun to change me in other ways. I was beginning to think that perhaps the phrase 'God's will' didn't quite mean what I had thought it did. I had thought it had been 'God's will' for me to go to Aubépine and that, by leaving, I was somehow not doing his will. But now I wondered about this. After all, God wasn't some sort of micro-manager, with an enormous blueprint of how life should pan out for each one of us. Perhaps there wasn't any blue print with a tiny section marked 'Noreen Mackey' on it. Perhaps the plan was much more flexible. Maybe it was quite simply a plan to bring each of us into freedom and into love, and how we got there was up to us. Maybe there were lots of paths to that place, and maybe God didn't mind which one we took. Looked at this way, joining Aubépine hadn't necessarily been God's specific will, and if so, leaving it hadn't somehow frustrated his plans. Perhaps I hadn't gone backwards at all; perhaps the whole thing had happened so that I could begin to learn to trust God, and to be ready to abandon my own plans when necessary. I would now try to carry that trust a little further, and launch out into the empty space that yawned in front of me, knowing that he was there even if I couldn't find him. I would cast myself into the void. Hugely cheered and filled with new energy, I looked around me at the place where I was. The quest was still in train; I had, after all, come further than I realised.

CHAPTER SEVEN

And all those that serve
Relate to me a thousand graces of thee,
And all wound me the more,
And something that they are stammering leaves me dying.

How quickly they passed, those few days in Manresa when I found happiness again! Somehow, prayer had once again become a place where I was at home, although the experience was very different from that of the Aubépine days. Once I let go of the need to control it, prayer took on its own life. Finbarr was right: all I had to do was show up at the trysting place. Now once again I couldn't get enough of it. In some strange way, I was being fed and satisfied by this experience of emptiness and non-presence.

'Which only goes to show,' Finbarr remarked when I told him this, 'that you can't really trust what you experience. God transcends your experiences, and can't be encompassed by them. So you interpret a presence that is too strong to take in as being absence. Strange, isn't it!'

What had been happening to my prayer, and why was I now finding some mysterious attraction in what had previously been frustrating and often unbearable? The scenario – at least the part about finding prayer frustrating – will be familiar to anyone who prays regularly. One's prayer life is precisely that: a life. Because it is living, it must either move forward or die. It can't just stay in a fixed position. When someone has been praying regularly, prayer tends to become simpler. Where it might have been necessary before to adopt various methods for easing one into that deep place – meditation, a mantra perhaps, the practice of 'following the breath' – there inevitably comes a time when these rather elaborate procedures are no longer needed. Familiarity with God in the depths of one's being has grown in such a way that a word or phrase, or an image (maybe not even a

religious image) or some scene of natural beauty will be suffi-
cient to draw the person into that quiet and wordless place
where deep exchanges take place between the person and God.

That stage can initially be peaceful and fulfilling but, again,
inevitably, if the person remains faithful and open to change,
other things will happen. The peace may be disturbed by unpleasant realisations about oneself. These have to be faced and
accepted, so that the person comes to a deeper knowledge of an
infinitely accepting God. Or, more subtly, the increasing close-
ness of God might produce an inner resistance born of fear that
may disguise itself as boredom. Or there may be other resist-
ances effectively preventing the praying person from hearing
what God wants to say. I think this last example is probably
what had been happening in my case. I had been holding on for
dear life to the belief that Véronique and Marie-Jeanne had been
wrong in sending me away from Aubépine, because if I once accepted that they were right, the consequences seemed to me too
horrible to contemplate.

What were these awful consequences, these mountains of the
mind that I couldn't bear to look at? There were, as I saw it, two
alternatives: either I had through my own fault lost a God-given
vocation, or I had only imagined that I had one in the first place,
and if I had imagined that, then how was I to trust anything that
had led up to it? So fear was setting up a huge resistance to hearing that Véronique and Marie-Jeanne had been right and, as
prayer was a place where I might have to face up to that fact, I
was, all unconsciously, making prayer unbearable for myself.

And now that I had faced it and accepted it, where were the
mountains? They had never been there at all. Chimeras, every
rocky one of them! Only now was I able to see that there had
been a third possibility all along: that God wanted me to be in
Aubépine precisely in order to undergo the very experiences I
had undergone, so that I could learn to trust him.

I found myself changing almost daily. The bitterness that had
burned in me like bile since leaving Aubépine had gone. I felt a
huge desire to see Véronique and Marie-Jeanne again, and to tell

them that I knew now they had been right. How had all this happened in such a sort time? I couldn't understand it. Finbarr could, though.

'God is free now to act in you, to begin to change you,' he explained. 'Your resistance is gone. When you place yourself before him in this sort of wordless prayer, you are totally at his disposition. You are there for him, not for yourself; because, as you have discovered, there isn't anything that appeals to the senses in this kind of prayer.'

This made sense, but still I was astonished by the ease with which it had all happened after so many months of angst. And now, as though I had been turned around and pointed in a different direction, other things also began to fall into place in my life.

The first thing that happened was that when I returned to the flat in Sydenham Road after the retreat in Manresa, a letter was waiting for me from the Civil Service Commission. It was in response to my application for the job of legal adviser in the Competition Authority, and it asked me to come for an interview on a date in late January. Taken aback, I suddenly realised I knew next to nothing about Irish competition law. Some quick education was called for. A visit to Hodges Figgis bookshop produced a textbook on the subject, and I got down to some cramming. I had about three weeks to bring myself up to scratch, and I didn't hold out too much hope for myself.

But I wasn't unduly perturbed. I was back on track as regards the quest, and I had now no doubt that other things would happen in their proper time. Armed with my new way of praying, I set about integrating it with my daily life. The morning prayer-time was once again a source of joy. The strange thing was that the more I persevered with the sort of 'non-prayer' that Finbarr had led me to, the more it began to feel like something – although not like anything that I could find words to describe. The place it brought me to was a secret place, a garden whose entrance was hidden even from me, so that sometimes when I found myself there I would wonder: how did I get here? I would sit down to prayer, and seem to face towards a blank wall. A moment of frustration would arise in me before I could bring myself to say: let it go, I'm here; nothing else matters. And then somehow, I would pass over or through the wall. Sometimes I would begin rather anxiously to try to trace the route that had taken me there, but inevitably, I would realise that I was outside the garden again. The nearest I came to a description of the process was in children's' literature. When I first read *Harry Potter*, the description of how to get to Platform 9¾ at Euston Station awoke in me a shock of delighted recognition. There was the blank wall; you walked towards it hopelessly and suddenly you had passed through it and were in another place, another dimension, able to board the Hogwarts Express and head off on a wonderful journey.

One of the first things I did after the retreat was to write to Véronique and Marie-Jeanne to tell them what had happened. Since my return to Ireland in October, I had made no contact with them except for a formally polite card at Christmas, although they had written me a number of anxious and affectionate little notes. Because I could not think of them without feelings of anger and bitterness, I had shut them out from my thoughts. Now I found myself thinking of them with great affection, and realising how difficult it must have been for them to do what they had done. I knew now that they been right, that the whole episode had been part of God's plan.

Within a week, a delighted response arrived, with an invitation to visit them as soon as I liked. Things were happening fast on another front too. The job interview went well, and in due course, I received a letter telling me, to my utter astonishment, that I had got the post. My starting date in the Competition Authority was in late March, so I decided to spend a few days in Aubépine before I began.

I had a strange sense of deja-vu at the railway station near Aubépine when I stepped off the TGV from Paris around four o'clock one Thursday evening some weeks later. Memories crowded upon me: I saw myself as I arrived at the same station on another March afternoon four years earlier, full of misgivings about my first visit to Aubépine. I saw myself again as I arrived there in January of 1996, apprehensive, but full of hope for the new life that I was about to begin with the community. And I could not but remember that sorrowful morning in September, just six months earlier, when I stood again in that same railway station, all my hopes and dreams in dust around my feet, or that other day, a few weeks later when I stopped there to change trains on my way from Chambarand to Metz. Suddenly, I remembered that now. Vividly, I saw myself, thin and shabby, still wearing the old gardening jeans in which I had left Aubépine, standing on the platform with my one suitcase on a warm September evening. I was feeling lost and vaguely panicky, wondering what my new home in Metz would be like, wishing desperately that I could put the clock back a few months and recapture everything I had lost, when suddenly, disbelievingly, I saw two small brown figures pushing through the crowd and waving.

'Véronique, Marie-Jeanne!' I said, confused, hugging them. 'What on earth are you doing here?'

'We came to see you off,' Marie-Jeanne explained. Weak tears sprang to my eyes. It was almost too much for my fragile composure. They had remembered the time I was to arrive at the station, and had come specially, just to see me. I had got on the Metz train fifteen minutes later with a raw aching pain inside me.

And now here I was once more, joyful, peaceful, looking forward to seeing all my old friends again. I searched my conscience: was there even the teeniest bit of regret, the smallest smidgen of angst or bitterness? No, I knew there wasn't. And this to me was a true miracle, and an indication of what God can do when we allow him to be God, and stop trying to interfere with his efforts to bring us into the freedom of his children.

Looking out the window of the taxi as it mounted the hill towards the monastery, I saw again the ploughed fields of my first visit, lit by the slanting rays of the evening sun. The sky was cloudless. I seemed always to be lucky with the weather when I visited Aubépine. The taxi swung around the last corner, and the little huddle of buildings came into view. As I was getting out of the car, the door of the *hôtellerie* burst open and Annette, the Guest Mistress, came running out, arms outstretched, beaming from ear to ear.

'*La voici, la grande fidèle!*' she cried.

I had got what very few people get in this life, the chance to start over again.

CHAPTER EIGHT

But how, o life, dost thou persevere,
Since thou livest not where thou livest,
And since the arrows make thee to die which thou receivest
From the conceptions of the Beloved which thou formest within thee?

For me, the job in the Competition Authority was going to be the real test of the authenticity of my prayer and of the new life I was trying to live, which was effectively the life of a contemplative in the middle of activity. While I was working for Bart Daly, I was able to regulate my day as I wanted. So long as the work was done, Bart didn't care when I did it. But now I would be subject to civil service hours, obliged to be in the office from nine to at least half past five every day. My various spiritual exercises – Mass, prayer times, recitation of parts of the office – would have to fit themselves around those times. Still rather rigid in my conception of how all this should be lived out, I began to plan out my timetable in some detail. Rise at six, an hour's prayer, recite Lauds, breakfast, leave the house at seven forty-five, Mass in the Pro-Cathedral at eight thirty, at the office by nine fifteen … I felt tired even thinking about it all, but I was convinced this was how it would have to be.

The Competition Authority was based on Parnell Square. This is not the most scenically attractive part of Dublin, so I was pleasantly surprised to find that the room allocated to me for my office looked out over the Garden of Remembrance and even had a view of the distant Dublin hills. On my first morning, the board members of the Authority (there were at that time four of them) took me out to lunch in Cassidy's Hotel on Cavendish Row. I was to be one of two legal advisers; the other, Daragh Daly, was also at the lunch. Much younger than I, he was totally at ease with the board members, while I felt awkward, not sure of my place in the hierarchy, or even whether there was a hierarchy at all. I was suddenly overcome with the feeling that I would never fit in there: they all chatted away about current affairs, politics and issues of competition, none of which I knew anything about. I wondered what Daragh and I would ever have in common. How would we get on? I felt dowdy and old; I was sure he must be disconcerted at the sight of his new colleague.

The first few days were difficult. My experiences in Aubépine had shaken both my self-image and my self-confidence. At every moment, I expected to be called to account, and was astonished when it didn't happen. Nobody criticised me, nobody seemed to feel that a mistake had been made in employing me, nobody threw any eggs. One day, Daragh, whose office was next door to mine, put his head around my door to ask my view about something. A bit hesitantly, I gave my opinion and was flabbergasted when he accepted it in preference to his own.

As the days and weeks wore on and it didn't look as if I was going to be sacked, I began to relax. I now had a job with a decent salary. I realised that I could think of getting somewhere a bit more spacious to live than the small flat in Sydenham Road. I enlisted Kay's help again, and we began to search the property columns in the daily papers. I needed an unfurnished apartment, as Sheelagh had all my furniture from Luxembourg in her house in Cork, but was now on the verge of marriage to Matthew, and would be moving. I thought that what I would like above all was an apartment with a view of the sea; but the rent on any coastal properties that were advertised was way above my budget. Then one day towards the end of April, while I was scanning the 'for rent' columns of the *Irish Times*, my eye fell on the following advertisement:

Unfurnished two-bedroom apartment near Sutton. Sea views. Rent, £650 per month.

I rang Kay immediately.

'The rent is above my limit', I told her, 'But all the same …'

'It can't do any harm to have a look at it', she said. 'Ring and make an appointment.'

A few days later she picked me up outside my office in Parnell Square and we set off northwards out of the city and along the coast road. The night before, Kay had done a bit of re-connoitring and had located the apartment block, so she knew exactly where it was. She told me now that it was on the corner of Kilbarrack Road, facing the sea. As we passed the Dart Station at Fairview, the sea and Howth Head came into view through the fine rain that was falling.

'That's the view from all the windows at the front of the building', Kay said. 'The advertisement said sea views, so pre-sumably the apartment we're going to see is at the front.'

We drove on through Clontarf, passing Manresa, the Jesuit centre. I suddenly realised that if I rented this apartment, I would be living nearby: it seemed like a good omen. We came to the junction at the Howth Road.

'Next corner,' said Kay, and there was the apartment block, set slightly at an angle to the coast road, oriented towards Howth Head. It was a 1970s red-brick building which had re-cently been modernised. Balconies decorated the façade; french windows leading on to them. 'Mariners Court', a large sign in the forecourt announced, with scant regard for commas. Lynn Truss would probably have refused to go any further, but I was prepared to overlook the odd missing punctuation mark so long as I could also overlook the sea.

'Kay, look!' I exclaimed. 'Balconies! I wonder if my apart-ment has one.'

'It isn't your apartment yet,' Kay reminded me, ever the voice of reason.

We drove in to the car park, and rang the doorbell. The agent was waiting to meet us and came down to bring us up. The apartment was on the first floor. The small, rather dark landing had just two doors opening off it. Putting her key in one, the agent pushed it open and we found ourselves in a little hallway, painted in neutral cream and stone tones. More doors opened off the hallway.

'This is the livingroom,' the agent said, opening the nearest door. Suddenly the hall was flooded with light. I followed the woman through and stopped, dazzled. A wall of glass faced the door and through it all you could see was the sea and Howth Head shining in the sun that was now forcing a path through the clouds. It was like being on a boat. The tide was in, and the cloud-filtered light shimmered and danced on the sea. Far out on the horizon some tiny yachts bobbed about. Dazed, I followed the agent who had slid back a door onto the balcony. As I stepped out after her, I heard Kay catch her breath behind me. I turned, and she grabbed my arm.

'Take it,' she mouthed urgently, 'Take it. It doesn't matter what it costs!'

I nodded agreement. I had already made up my mind. Standing there on the balcony, doing rapid sums in my head, I knew I was a lost cause.

In the end, I needn't have worried about the cost, because I was able to bargain down the rent on the basis that the apartment was unfurnished. Ireland is a country of property-owners, and it is quite difficult to let an unfurnished apartment. People who had their own furniture usually had their own property too. I was the exception, having been obliged to purchase furniture in Luxembourg, a country where the reverse is true. I later discovered that the Mariners Court apartment had been on the market for quite a while; the owners had just decided to take it off and furnish it when I turned up. They were so glad to let it that a rent reduction wasn't a problem. I moved in in mid-May 1998. Two old friends from the Law Library, Peter and Jane, came to help with the move and that evening we had an impromptu picnic on the balcony, with champagne brought by Peter and finger food contributed by Jane. It was a glorious evening. As the sun set behind the building and the moon rose over the sea, we watched from the balcony, cardboard cups of champagne in hand, as the ferry from Holyhead made its slow creeping way across the Dublin Bay into Dún Laoghaire.

After Peter and Jane had gone home, I continued to sit there. My mind wandered back over the events of the previous five years. The whole adventure had begun on another balcony, on another summer evening, in another country. It was while sitting on the balcony of my apartment in Luxembourg that I had experienced the absence of God from my life, and at the same moment, discovered that in fact he had never been absent at all. This revelation, this epiphany, had caused me to set out on a quest that was geographical as well as spiritual, taking me as it did to Aubépine in France, and from there to Chambarand, to Metz, back to Luxembourg, and finally, back to Ireland, to this balcony where I now sat watching the moon and the dark sea. A stillness crept over everything; a stillness that seemed to come from that inner core where prayer sometimes led me. Was I approaching it at last, I wondered, that 'place where none appeared'? But I knew enough now to know that that elusive place was never where I thought I would find it. It probably was not here either.

Seeking my love, I will go o'er yonder mountains and banks;
I will neither pluck the flowers nor fear the wild beasts;
I will pass by the mighty and cross the frontiers,

wrote John of the Cross. There are resting places, but they must never be confused with the secret place where the quest ends. After the experience on the balcony in Luxembourg, I had believed that I would find it in Aubépine. I had been wrong. Aubépine was not the place where I was to stay; it was a place along the way, a place where I would learn, where I would find tools and support for the rough places ahead. I had to go further. But for some months after I had left, during the period when I thought a huge mistake had been made, I had re-examined what I had taken to be signs and portents along the route and concluded that I had been wrong about them. One in particular, which had seemed like a direct message from God at the time, then began to seem nothing more than an illusion.

It had happened in the Church of St Michel in Dijon, where, on the way back to Luxembourg from an early visit to Aubépine, I had gone to visit the relics of Blessed Elisabeth of the Trinity, a Carmelite of the early twentieth century. My feelings were in turmoil, because it was during that visit that I had realised that I wanted to join the community. It seemed an impossible step to take: for one thing, I didn't believe the community would accept me. I had attempted to live the Carmelite life before, when I was much younger, and it hadn't worked then. Why should it be any different now? Praying before Blessed Elisabeth's relics, I noticed a large book open on a stand nearby, where people could write their intentions. A notice beside it said that the intentions entered in the book each day would be prayed for at Mass in the church the following morning. I wrote: 'Please Elisabeth, bring me back to Carmel.' When I had done this, a great peace filled me, as if I had now done everything possible and could leave the whole matter safely in another's hands.

The following morning I attended the 9 o'clock Mass in St Michel, acutely conscious that my intention was one of those being prayed for during the Mass. The opening stages of the liturgy unfolded and a reader went to the lectern to read the first lesson. It was from the Prophet Jeremiah. Only half comprehending the biblical French, I was suddenly jolted fully into awareness by words that seemed to be addressed directly to me. *'Si tu reviens'*, I heard, *'si je te fais revenir, tu reprendras ton service devant moi.'* 'If you come back, if I bring you back, then you will take up your service again in my presence.'

It was a moment when time stopped. I had not the slightest doubt that I had heard the word of God addressed to me and at the deepest level, I believed it would come true. My subsequent acceptance by the community and my entrance into the Carmel of Aubépine had only been, as far as I was concerned, a confirmation of the validity of that experience. God had brought me back as he had promised and I was once again taking up service in his presence.

And then it all came to an end. I left Aubépine. God's word had not proved true. Yet that could not be. God's word must always prove true. I was forced then to the inescapable conclusion that this had not been God's word at all, but just my own overheated imagination. I was desolate. Filled with the idea of joining the community at Aubépine, I had been convinced that God had been telling me I would take up my service again in his presence in the Carmelite order. I had not even considered the possibility that it might have another meaning.

Now, however, I was learning that there are different ways of interpreting things. Sitting alone on the balcony on that first evening in Mariners Court, I thought about all that had happened since I had returned to Ireland. I was certainly consciously living my life now in God's presence. Maybe that was what the experience in Dijon had meant. Maybe the Carmelite life had never been an essential element of the quest. Struck suddenly by the huge implications of this for all that had gone before, especially for what it meant in relation to my first essay of the religious life, I felt overwhelmed. Mariners Court was already bringing its own revelations. Little did I suspect that even greater ones were in store.

CHAPTER NINE

Since thou hast wounded this heart,
Wherefore didst thou not heal it?
And wherefore, having robbed me of it, hast thou left it thus
And takest not the prey that thou hast spoiled?

All during that first year back in Ireland, prayer, and my understanding of how the quest should be followed by me were deepening. I felt a great need for solitude, so that the understanding that was glimmering at the edges of my consciousness could develop. Sometimes I felt I was at the brink of a huge breakthrough, but always it proved elusive. When the summer came, I wanted to take my annual leave in some quiet place where I could sit undisturbed face to face with mystery. I decided to go to the Aran Islands.

The Aran Islands are situated off the west coast of Ireland, in the middle of Galway Bay. There are three islands: Inismor (the largest) Inismaan and Inisheer. Gaelic is still the first language of the islanders. Ruins of early Christian monasteries and even more ancient fortifications are dotted about the landscape, giving the visitor a sense of having stepped back in time. You can take the ferry from Rossaveal in Connemara or from Doolin in County Clare – a wonderful way to travel on a fine summer's day, with the wind in your hair and the sunlight flashing on the water – or you can fly over from Connemara Regional Airport. I chose the latter; an adventure in itself. Not only your luggage, but you yourself have to be weighed before boarding the tiny nine-seater plane. I found myself sitting directly behind the pilot. Turning around to check his passengers before take-off, he noticed that my seat-belt was too loosely fastened. Frowning, he leaned over the back of his seat and tightened it. Here was novelty indeed!

The eight-minute flight is, as far as I know, the shortest scheduled flight in Europe. The little plane flies low over the

ocean, affording glorious views of the Galway coastline and of
the Islands themselves. That particular day we were not flying
direct to Inismor; we were going to make a brief stop at
Inismaan to take on passengers. We landed. Three passengers
got on; two elderly women and a man who could not have
weighed less than twenty stone. The pilot got out and began to
reorganise us. It was necessary to distribute us differently to accommodate the unexpected additional weight. All in new seats,
we took off again. As we approached Inismor, the pilot made an
announcement over his completely unnecessary sound system.

'Passengers are requested not to open the doors until the
plane has landed!'

After the weight-distributing experience, I wasn't absolutely
certain that he was joking.

Landing on Inismor also has its unique appeal. Our plane
was waved down to the runway by a lone woman accompanied
by a dog. This woman and her husband run the tiny airport between them. When we had disembarked, we waited on the tarmac while she and the pilot unloaded our luggage. It was like
getting off a long distance bus.

The guesthouse I was to stay in had been recommended by
Kay. Called Árd Éinne, it was situated on a headland about five
minutes walk from the airport at the opposite end of the island
to Kilronan, the principal town. Árd Éinne was the perfect place
for a seeker after solitude. Every day after breakfast, I walked
the few miles to Kilronan where I bought some bread, cheese
and fruit. Then I made my way back to the headland, past Árd
Éinne and across fields dotted with rabbit warrens until I
reached the cliffs. There on the edge of the Atlantic ocean I sat
and watched the ballet danced by the huge foaming waves as
they rose and fell, rose and fell, in an eternal sequence against
the opposite cliffs of Inismaan and I thought and read and
prayed until it was time to cross once more the rabbit fields,
where white tails flashed and bobbed in the long rays of the setting sun as the rabbits dived for cover at my approach.

During the solitude of those days on Inismor, I came gradually to the realisation that I wanted to make some formal commitment of my life to God. If I had remained in Aubépine, I would have made a profession of the three vows of poverty, chastity and obedience, signifying that my whole life belonged exclusively to the One I was seeking. I knew now that community life wasn't for me; Aubépine had proved that beyond the least shadow of doubt. But I could think of no other way of totally committing my life to God. I had, it is true, made a commitment to a life of celibacy even before I had joined Aubépine, but that was a purely private vow. I had made it in the summer of 1994 as a direct response to a call I believed I had experienced when reading a passage from the Song of Songs some months earlier. I took this vow very seriously, but I wanted to do something more, something that would be recognised by the church as committing me irrevocably to Christ. I was in a quandary.

I puzzled over the problem unsuccessfully for some time. During a visit to Manresa towards the end of the year, I told Finbarr Lynch what I had been thinking about. Finbarr had by now become my spiritual director and I was in the habit of visiting him once every two months or so. He asked me if I had ever thought of making a commitment to a life of consecrated virginity. I didn't know what he was talking about, so he explained that the life of consecrated virginity (or celibacy, as I prefer to call it) is the oldest form of consecrated life, restored as a special rite of the church after the second Vatican Council. The consecrated woman lives this vocation completely in the world. She wears no special garb (except a ring) and has no special title. She earns her own living. She is free to choose her own way to serve the church, according to her natural gifts and talents. However, prayer is a particularly important part of the life of such a woman, and it was the emphasis on this that attracted me when Finbarr told me about it.

I made some enquiries and found that I should contact Father Martin Hogan, who was at that time based in Clonliffe College. He was the spiritual director of consecrated women in the Dublin diocese. I went to see him and told him my history.

He suggested that I undergo a period of discernment with a view to making a commitment after a year or eighteen months. He proposed setting up a small group of people, of which he would be one, to help me with the discernment process. He suggested a nun he knew who was attached to Mater Dei Institute as another member, and he asked me to propose a third person, who ideally, would be a lay person: someone who had known me for a long time, who was a person of spirituality, and who would sympathise with the lifestyle I was proposing to lead. The idea was that I would meet regularly with the members of the group on a one-to-one basis, and that the group as a whole would assemble towards the end of the year to pool their views on whether or not I should proceed.

I thought for a long time about who I might ask to be the third member of the group. It was, I knew, a burden to ask anyone to take on. I could think of only one person outside of my family who fulfilled almost all the requirements, and with whom at the same time I would feel comfortable having the sort of discussions that were envisaged. That person was Irene Dunne.

Irene and I go back a long way. We met on our first day in secondary school, two excited twelve-year-olds feeling that life was now really beginning. It was Irene who had inadvertently been instrumental in causing me to set out on the quest. When we were both sixteen, she had lent me a book about the Carmelite life that had been the direct cause of my discovery of the writings of St John of the Cross, a discovery that had influenced my whole life.

Irene always had natural leadership qualities. At school, she was head girl when we were in sixth year. She was bright and talented and everyone expected her to go far. It was a huge shock to everyone in the class when, shortly before our Leaving Certificate exam, Irene announced that she was going to enter the novitiate of the Holy Faith congregation, the congregation which ran our school. There too her leadership qualities have been recognised, and she has fulfilled various onerous responsibilities over the years.

It was, then, natural that Irene should come into my head as an appropriate person to join the discernment group. She knew me well, and indeed her friendship had been a huge support around the time of my departure from my first essay at religious life, in the 1970s. The only problem was that she was not a layperson. However, I sorted this out with Father Hogan and then the only question was whether Irene would have the time to take on this extra burden. She didn't hesitate for a moment, so the discernment group was constituted and my year of probation began.

Around this time I began to experience a growing desire to write about my time in Aubépine. One evening, I sat down at the computer and tried to start. I found it very difficult. My main problem at that time was to find a written voice of my own; one that I liked the sound of and that was at the same time authentic. Not surprisingly, I tended to write like a lawyer, in a very formal and correct way that didn't sound good to my ear. That evening, I played about a bit with various beginnings, and I didn't like any of them. Then I thought: how do I feel when I think about Aubépine? Nostalgic? Yes, a little. Bittersweet? That too. I thought of the opening of one of my favourite books, *Brideshead Revisited*, and could almost hear the dreamy voice of Jeremy Irons reading the opening lines:

I have been here before,' I said; I had been there before; first with Sebastian more than twenty years ago on a cloudless day in June, when the ditches were creamy with meadowsweet and the air heavy with all the scents of summer …

That was the voice I was looking for, that voice of nostalgic remembrance of things past. Listening to it, I started to write:

Aubépine! The name still evokes longings deep in my heart. I have only to close my eyes, find that inner space of silence, and I am back there once again.

Although I didn't know it then, I had begun to write a book.

However, beginning was one thing; continuing was something else entirely. Having written what would eventually become the prologue of *The Secret Ladder*, I found I had no idea where the book was going to go from there. Indeed, I didn't even know where the story should start. From time to time, over the weeks and months that followed, I jotted down incidents that had happened during my time at Aubépine. They were usually light-hearted vignettes of community life, and I could see no way of linking them together to make a coherent whole. Eventually, I lost enthusiasm for the project and put it to one side, although I carefully filed all the attempts away on my computer, in a folder called simply 'Aubépine'. Maybe I would go back to it someday.

CHAPTER TEN

Quench thou my griefs,
Since none suffices to remove them,
And let mine eyes behold thee
Since thou art their light
And for thee alone I wish to have them.

Meanwhile, other events were taking place both externally and internally. At that time, the Competition Authority was a very small organisation of about twenty people and, although independent in its work, it was nevertheless for employment purposes part of the civil service. There were seven or eight professional staff, mainly economists. Daragh and I were the only lawyers. The remainder of the staff were career civil servants, but the economists and lawyers were all on temporary contracts. This state of affairs was unsatisfactory, and the professional staff made representations to the board seeking to be made permanent, and to have our positions upgraded (we were all at that time treated for salary and other purposes as though we were assistant principal officers in the civil service). The board members were sympathetic, but could do nothing without government sanction, which at that time was not forthcoming. The inevitable happened, as one by one the professional staff left for more secure or better-paid employment. I successfully applied for a job as parliamentary counsel in the Office of the Attorney General, but agreed to give three months notice to the Authority to enable it to replace me. I was sorry to go. I had enjoyed the work and I had made friends there.

One Friday evening only a couple of weeks after having secured the new job, the phone rang as I was tidying up my desk preparatory to leaving for the weekend. I picked up the receiver and a voice informed me that the Secretary General of the Department of Enterprise, Trade and Employment would like to speak to me. I was puzzled. I had met the Secretary General only once, on the day I had started work with the Authority, and I couldn't imagine why he wanted to speak to me.

I waited. A man's voice came on the line.

'Noreen,' he began cheerfully, 'your name has been mentioned today in high places!'

A faint suspicion began to form in my mind. I said nothing.

'Yes,' the voice continued, 'I've just come from a meeting with the Attorney General and the Tánaiste and we were talking about you.'

My suspicion hardened. This was not the Secretary General at all. It was my old friend Peter, barrister-at-law and practical joker extraordinaire. He was no doubt going to go on to tell me that I had been appointed to some high office, and would then fall around the place laughing when I bit the bait. It was not the first time that I had been at the receiving end of one of his jokes. The day of my move to Mariners Court, I was waiting in the Ballsbridge flat for him. He had promised to come to help with the move. The removal men were already there and everything was in chaos. The telephone rang. With some difficulty, I unearthed it from under a pile of books on the floor.

'May I speak to Noreen Mackey?' a polite male voice enquired. I identified myself.

'I'm ringing from RTÉ radio', the voice went on. 'I understand you are the legal adviser with the Competition Authority?'

Alarmed, I admitted that I was.

'Ah', said the voice warmly. 'Good. I'm a researcher with the Pat Kenny show, and I'd like to ask you your view of the latest EU block exemption.'

The latest EU block exemption? It was the first I had heard of it. I had no idea there was a new one, much less what view I held concerning it.

'I'm afraid you'll have to ring the Competition Authority and speak to someone there,' I said, with what firmness I could muster. 'I'm on a day off today. How did you get my number, anyway?'

'I got it from the Competition Authority, actually,' the voice said. 'That was naturally the first place I rang, but they told me that you were the person to speak to, and they gave me this number.'

Panic-stricken, I cursed the Authority interiorly, while at the same time realising that I had reached the end of the line. I was unmasked for the fraud I was. I knew nothing about any new block exemption. I would have to tell this appalling researcher so and no doubt that would be the end of my job at the Competition Authority. I took a deep breath, and was about to come clean when I heard a peculiar sound at the other end of the line. It sounded as if the researcher was quietly choking.

'Hello?' I said rather anxiously.

The sound came again. It sounded like … could it possibly be … was the man actually laughing? And was that a second person I could hear in the background, making similar choking noises? Suddenly it all became clear to me.

'Peter, is that you?'

It was Peter indeed, egged on by my other friend Jane whose background hysterics I could now hear quite plainly. So it was only natural that I should, on that June evening in my office, believe that he was at it again. I smiled grimly. He wouldn't catch me out this time. But just as I was about to unmask him, the voice continued:

'We need a barrister to act as a third inspector in an investigation under the Companies legislation in relation to a fairly high profile company.'

Suddenly it didn't sound like Peter any more. I listened, and as the Secretary General continued to speak, I realised with a huge sense of shock that I, who only a year earlier had thought I would never be able to work as a lawyer again, was now being asked to undertake a government investigation into widespread tax evasion among prominent Irish citizens during the late 1970s and early 1980s.

The Ansbacher affair, as it became known, is really a misnomer, and it has caused no small amount of grief to Ansbacher Bank, a reputable company, to find its name associated with the infamous tax scandal. It should more correctly have been called the Guinness Mahon Cayman Trust affair, because that was the original name of the company at the heart of it. The brainchild of

Desmond Traynor, one of the directors of Guinness & Mahon, a respected merchant bank in Dublin, GMCT (as it was known) was set up in the Cayman islands in the early 1970s. It was bought after some years as an offshore subsidiary by Ansbacher Bank, which renamed it – no doubt to its everlasting regret – Ansbacher (Cayman) Limited.

The investigation in which I was to play a part was established in order to find out whether this offshore company had breached any laws. Suspicions had arisen through evidence given to another tribunal that the bank had been used over a period of years to conceal funds belonging to wealthy Irish clients – funds upon which Irish tax might not have been paid.

Listening to the Secretary General explaining this, my heart started to fail me. What on earth did I know about banking or taxation? Answer: nothing. I tried to get this across to the man who was speaking, but he waved it aside.

'We already have two proposed Inspectors, one of whom is an accountant,' he explained. 'The other is the former President of the High Court, Mr Justice Declan Costello. There will also be a back-up staff of accountants, so don't worry about that aspect of things. You'll deal with the legal part of the enquiry.'

I wasn't convinced, but he talked on encouragingly. He told me I didn't have to decide immediately, but could have the night to think it over. He had spoken to Jim Hamilton, my future boss in the Attorney General's office (and now Director of Public Prosecutions) who had said I could ring him that evening to talk about it. The Attorney General's office had agreed to second me to the investigation for as long as it took. The conversation went on for over half an hour, and when it ended with my promise to give my answer in the morning, my head was spinning.

That night, I spent a long time on the phone. I rang Jim Hamilton, who encouraged me. I rang Kay, who also encouraged me and Finbarr Lynch in Manresa, who, as I had known he would, suggested that I pray about it. I didn't sleep much that night. By the following morning, I had arrived at a position where I felt that unless there was some very good reason why I should refuse, then I should accept. And as I could think of no good reason for refusing, I rang the Secretary General and accepted, thus precipitating an entirely new stage of the quest.

For I knew that nothing in my life was happening by chance. I was certain that I had been guided in every step I had taken since the evening on the balcony in Luxembourg where I had committed my life irrevocably to the quest for God. I had followed strange and tortuous paths, but even those which had seemed to lead to emptiness and to the desert turned out to be the right ones for that part of the journey. The desert had blossomed, and ways had opened up where I could see none. So it would be with this Ansbacher investigation, which, at first sight, didn't seem to have very much to do with God. But I knew now that everything had to do with God because quite simply, we are part of his creation. 'In him we live, move and have our being,' said St Paul, preaching to the Greeks in Athens. If this is so – and it is – then every aspect of our life and loves and work is intimately concerned with God.

Many years later, I read a remarkable book called *God in All Things* by Gerard Hughes which stresses this very point. Hughes talks about what he calls our 'split spirituality' – the phenomenon which causes us to behave as if we could nurture the spiritual side of us in isolation from the physical.

We speak of natural and supernatural, spiritual and material, eternal and temporal, sacred and secular, grace and nature. While these can be useful distinctions, they can easily be misunderstood to indicate that there are two layers of reality: the natural, material layer, and the supernatural, spiritual layer. The conscientious Christian is encouraged to consider the supernatural to be of greater importance than the natural, the spiritual as more important than the material.

To underline the consequences of such a misunderstanding, Hughes asks us to imagine that we are heading off on a long-haul flight. Which, he asks us, would we prefer: a pilot whose mind is on God and spiritual things, but not on material things, or a pilot whose attention during the flight is concentrated on flying the plane safely? This points out that sort of 'double think' that our split spirituality induces: spiritual is more important than material, but not if our life is in danger.

The Ansbacher investigation got under way the following September. As evidence, mainly documentary, mounted up, I sometimes wondered despairingly how we were ever going to reduce it all to a written report at the end. Part of the problem was that the most probative evidence was in the Cayman Islands, where it was protected by strict secrecy laws. Without that evidence, our task of deduction was much more difficult and involved painstaking linking of documents with the oral evidence of those witnesses who were still alive. None of these witnesses knew more than a part of the scheme. That, in fact, was its strength.

In the hope of somehow getting around the Cayman Island secrecy laws, we hired lawyers in Grand Cayman and initiated litigation in the Cayman courts. In furtherance of this, I travelled alone to Grand Cayman early in the investigation. Mindful of the need to keep down costs, I did the round trip in four days, two of which were spent coming and going. The journey was in three stages: Dublin-London, London-Miami and Miami-Grand Cayman. The flight from Miami arrived in Grand Cayman at 9.00 pm. We had flown through a violent thunderstorm, throughout which I had kept my head down and my eyes covered, ignoring all the exhortations of the enthusiastic pilot to look out the window at the spectacular displays of forked lightning. We landed in what seemed the middle of nowhere. I could dimly make out the shape of an unlighted building as we disembarked into a tropical night whose damp heat felt like a blanket across my face. As our little group of passengers walked across the tarmac, we were caught in a sudden blaze of light from huge spotlights, and at the same moment, a brass band burst forth. To my utter amazement, marching towards us from the building came a colourful group of pirates, brandishing cutlasses and carrying glasses of rum which they proceeded to offer us. We had arrived at the beginning of Pirates' Week, a festival that occurs every October. Typical of the rather cavalier attitude of the Cayman Islands to numbers, Pirates' Week actually lasts eleven days – just as the famous Seven Mile Beach is in fact nine and a half miles long.

A bit dazed by this not inappropriate reception, given what I was there to investigate, I made my way through immigration to the arrivals area, where someone from our lawyers' firm was to meet me. As I looked around the crowd a young man made his way across to me and introduced himself. His car was waiting outside ready to bring me to my hotel. We walked a short distance down the road to where a magnificent, bright red BMW was parked. As we drove off into the tropical night with the hood down, the air heavy with the perfume of some unknown blossom, I surreptitiously pinched myself. Only two and a half years earlier I had been a nun in an enclosed monastery in Aubépine, believing that I was there for ever, that I would never again see anything outside the monastery. Never, in my wildest dreams, could I have imagined myself driving in a red sports car across a tropical island on my way to carry out an investigation into secret bank accounts on behalf of the Irish government. *Ex-nun carries out government investigation into secret bank accounts on Caribbean island!* I thought, stifling a grin. Sometimes life is so strange that if you turned it into a novel people would refuse to read it, on the ground that the story was too far-fetched!

CHAPTER ELEVEN

Reveal thy presence
And let the vision of thee and thy beauty slay me;
Behold, the affliction of love is not cured
Save by thy presence and thy form.

The new millennium was ushered in by a firework display on the Dublin quays that could be seen for miles around the coast. My sister Eileen, my brother-in-law Aiden and I stood on the balcony of my apartment in Mariners Court watching the extraordinary effects the lights in the sky produced in the water below. At times it looked as though the sea was exploding, as the flashes and flames and bursts of coloured stars were replicated on its surface.

'You are so lucky to live by the sea,' Eileen said.

She was right. I was very happy there. The balcony with its view of the sea had filled the empty space left by the Luxembourg balcony with its woods and hills. Apart from the fact that my prayer life had revived in Mariners Court, other happy events had taken place in that apartment. High among them in order of importance and of happiness had been the marriage of Eileen and Aiden a few months earlier. True, the marriage itself had not taken place there, but Eileen had stayed there the night before, and we had had a champagne breakfast the following morning. I reminded her of it now.

'I'll never forget the sight that met me that morning when I came into the living room,' she said.

'And I'll never forget the look on your face when you saw it.'

We were silent for a moment, remembering that most perfect of mornings. I had got up early in order to decorate the living room and prepare for the forthcoming breakfast. We were expecting the rest of the family, the bridesmaids, flower girl and one or two close friends. I drew back the curtains and looked out. The tide was full, and the sea was a deep blue, reflecting a cloudless September sky. Howth Head gleamed in the morning sun, every field and house distinctly visible in the clear air – a little too visible for comfort, perhaps; high visibility often meant rain to come. But for the moment it was perfect. I heard Eileen's bedroom door open and close and then her sudden indrawn breath as she entered the room and the vista burst upon her sight. The decorations and floral arrangements within couldn't even begin to compare with the splendour that had been laid on outside.

I thought now how much I would love to stay there, but I could not afford to buy it and I knew the time had come to buy something, if I was ever going to do it. For the Irish property market had gone completely crazy and house prices in Dublin were rapidly rising beyond the reach of many first-time buyers.

I had never owned any property. Before I went to work in Luxembourg in 1993, my accountant had on many occasions advised me to think of buying even a small flat. I had postponed the idea out of fear of being unable to keep up mortgage repayments on the uncertain income I was making at the Bar. But by the end of 1992, I was seriously considering purchasing a small apartment in a new city-centre development on Bachelors Walk. A one-bedroom apartment there cost around £IR 30,000 at that time. But then the opportunity arose to go to work at the European Court of Justice in Luxembourg. I didn't hesitate about accepting the job – it was, after all, a once in a lifetime opportunity – but I was in a quandary as to what I should do about the proposed purchase. Should I go ahead, and then rent it out to tenants for the few years that I would be away? In the end, being a landlord at long distance seemed more trouble than it was worth and I never made the purchase. How I regretted that decision now! The apartment would by now have been worth three times its price, and its sale would have allowed me to put down a deposit on a much nicer place. Instead, I was totally dependent on the small sum I had saved, and would, as a result, have to take out a very big mortgage. Prices were rising all the time and I knew that it was now or never.

I had already, in a half-hearted sort of way, done a bit of house-hunting the previous autumn, urged on by an anxious Kay who was concerned at the way I was frittering money away on the rent of an expensive apartment. We had seen a house advertised on a road only five minutes walk away from Mariners Court. It was just about within my price range and we had gone to look at it. It was a semi-detached two story house with a gabled roof, at the end of a terrace of similar houses. It had gardens back and front, wildly tangled and overgrown, but inside, in spite of the fact that it was over fifty years old, it was pleasantly modern. An extension had been built at some time and this housed a bright kitchen-cum-dining room whose french windows opened on to the wilderness outside. But most importantly from my point of view, it was in an area that I had grown to love, with its proximity to the sea, to St Anne's Park in Raheny – and, of course, to Manresa. I had made an offer for the house straight away. Two days later, the estate agent phoned to say that someone else had made a better offer, one that I was unable to cap. That, for the time being, had been the full extent of my house-hunting.

In mid-January of 2000, I started out in earnest and within three weeks I was almost in despair. Houses seemed to be rising in price by the week. There was no longer the faintest hope of finding anything I could afford in the area around Mariners Court. I began to look further afield without any greater success. One Saturday, returning home on the bus after a particularly discouraging and depressing viewing of three former council houses, none of which had been modernised in any way, I opened the *Irish Times* at the property ads in what was now almost a reflex action. I wondered why I was bothering. Thursday was the day for the main property ads in the *Irish Times*; I had found nothing then and I wasn't likely to do so now. Scanning the few columns, my eye was suddenly caught by the word 'Firhouse'. Startled, I looked more closely.

'Firhouse. Two, three and four bedroom houses from £IR128,000,' it said.

I couldn't believe it. There were three noteworthy things about this advertisement: the possibility of a two-bedroom house (just the right size for me); the starting price (I could rise at a pinch to £IR130,000) and the location. I knew Firhouse very well indeed. It was in Firhouse that the Carmel I had entered when I was eighteen was located. I still visited it from time to time, and the idea that I might be able to buy a house there seemed somehow part of everything that had been happening. I would be coming full circle.

I rang the estate agent on Monday, and on Tuesday evening Kay and I were on the road again, heading along the M50 towards Firhouse to view the house that was to become my home. I liked it immediately. It was a tiny bungalow, set in a secluded cul-de-sac of other bungalows and larger two-storey houses. I made an offer, it was accepted, and matters were decided. I would move into my own house in April.

But before that, one of the most profound experiences of my life was to take place in Mariners Court.

CHAPTER TWELVE

O Crystalline fount,
If on that thy silvered surface
Thou wouldst of a sudden form the eyes desired
Which I bear outlined in my inmost parts!

There were two bedrooms in the apartment in Mariners Court. The first thing I had done when I moved in was to turn the smaller one into a prayer room. Having a room to which I could go in order to pray was a luxury, and I made full use of it. The room was simply arranged. It contained a prayer stool and an icon standing on a pile of books over which I had draped a silk scarf. In front of this I arranged green trailing plants, candles, and sometimes flowers. The room also contained a sofa bed, so that I could turn it back into a bedroom and accommodate friends when necessary.

Every morning, before I went to work, I spent some time in this room with its peaceful view of the green lawn behind our building and of the old oak trees which divided the property from that of the Sisters of St Joseph next door. I went there again in the evening after work, to say the office of evening prayer, and sometimes too to say night prayer or to do some *lectio divina* – meditative reading from the scriptures. It became my refuge, my sanctuary, my place for encountering Mystery. And it was in that quiet place that one of the central experiences of my life occurred.

It happened during prayer one morning in the early spring of 2000. It was a day like any other. I have never been one for leaping out of bed in the mornings (apart from a short period in Aubépine when my competitive nature drove me to attempt to get downstairs in the morning before Angèle, my fellow-novice – an attempt invariably doomed to disappointment). That day, I got out of bed with the same difficulty as usual, groaning as I stretched stiff limbs. (Was it my imagination, or were they just that little bit stiffer than they had been two years ago? Since I had turned fifty, I had become increasingly conscious of the occasional aches and pains – not to mention the wrinkles and creases – that portended the inevitable breaking down of the whole structure.) It was still dark, although the first birds were beginning to sing as, bleary-eyed, I drew back the curtains to examine the weather. It wasn't raining; that was something at least. I showered, made the bed and went into the prayer room. Lighting the candles, I knelt down and began, as I always did, with a prayer to the Holy Spirit.

Come, Holy Spirit, fill the hearts of your faithful, and enkindle in them the fire of your love. Send forth, O Lord, your Spirit, and they shall be created, and you will renew the face of the earth. O God, who by the light of the Holy Spirit did instruct the hearts of the faithful, grant, we beseech you, that by the light of the same Spirit, we may have a right understanding in all things and ever rejoice in his holy consolations, through Christ our Lord. Amen.

I sat back on the prayer stool. The birds had finished their warming-up exercises and were now in full voice outside the window, where a dim line of light was becoming visible at the point where the curtains met. I closed my eyes. A project I was involved in at work intruded itself into my consciousness. My knee ached. There was an annoying itch in the middle of my backbone, where I couldn't quite reach it. I just knew it was going to be one of those days when I was going to be distracted, when I would be tempted away from prayer, like John Donne, 'for the noise of a Flie, for the ratling of a Coach, for the whining of a door …'. Sighing, (where were those holy consolations that I was supposed to be rejoicing in?) I tried to let go of anxiety, to stop concentrating, to stop trying so hard. I was not the only one present at this tryst, as Finbarr so often reminded me. It was not *my* prayer; it was *our* prayer.

I tried some breathing exercises. I breathed in and out, trying to concentrate on nothing but the movements of my lungs.

In, out …

In and out …

In. And out...

Time began to slow down. Slowly, slowly, I felt that sense of spiralling inward and downward to another place, another dimension, petals of a flower folding in upon itself. Gradually, a great silence enveloped me, and a deep peace. Then sweetly, gently, without any shock or sense of intrusion, a verse of poetry presented itself whole and entire to my mind, almost as though I were listening to someone reciting it:

O crystalline fount, If on that thy silvered surface,
Thou wouldst of a sudden form the eyes desired,
Which I bear outlined in my inmost parts

And suddenly, with a huge shock, I knew it was true.

I knew as clearly – more clearly – than if I could see them, I knew beyond all possibility of doubt, that those 'eyes' were indeed outlined in my inmost parts.

As suddenly as it had begun, the experience ended. I opened my eyes. I was back in the little room in Mariners Court, but where had I been? I stood up and pulled aside the curtain. Nothing had changed exteriorly except that dawn had broken, and a hazy greyness lay over the lawn. I knew that if I walked across the apartment to the front of the building, I would see a streak of light on the horizon, brightening the otherwise dark waters of the full morning tide. And yet something so momentous had occurred that really all I could say about it right then was that it was momentous. What it actually was, or meant, I didn't know.

I went back to the prayer stool, sat down and tried to retrace what had happened. There had been a deep silence, and then I had heard or remembered (but was it really either?) a verse of poetry. I had recognised the verse immediately. It was from the *Spiritual Canticle* of my old friend, John of the Cross. But I hadn't realised I knew it by heart. While I could repeat word for word many of the verses of that wonderful poem, this was not one of them. It had never spoken to me as had, for example, the two radiant stanzas where all life and love and nature is described as being found in the Beloved, and which, even as I write them now, work their old magic:

My Beloved, the mountains, the solitary wooded valleys,
The strange islands, the sonorous rivers,
The whisper of the amorous breezes.

The tranquil night, at the time of the rising of the dawn,
The silent music, the sounding solitude, the supper that recreates and enkindles love.

I repeated the other verse to myself again 'O crystalline fount ...' Certainly I seemed to have it off by heart now. I wondered if I had it correctly. Rising, I went into the living room and took the *Spiritual Canticle* from the bookshelves. It was the same copy I had stumbled upon that evening in Luxembourg six years earlier, when another verse of the same poem had changed my life forever. I looked at that other verse again now in passing:

Whither hast thou hidden thyself, and hast left me, O Beloved, to my sighing?
Thou didst flee like the hart, having wounded me: I went out after thee, calling, and thou wert gone.

Was what had now taken place the answer to that question I had asked that evening in Luxembourg? Had the Beloved told me where he was hiding? If so, did this mean I had reached the end of the quest? Somehow, I didn't really think the quest was over. And yet ... I had asked him to tell me where he had hidden himself, and now I knew the answer. But I felt dissatisfied. Somehow, what had happened was more than an answer to a question. I flicked forward through the verses of the long poem until I found the one I was looking for. Yes, word, for word, it was exactly as it had come into my mind. I read a little of John's commentary on the verse. The 'eyes desired' are the eyes of the Beloved, desired by the person who is seeking him. The crystalline fount is faith, and the person seeking the Beloved is asking to be allowed to see those eyes which faith tells her are engraved in her inmost being.

I returned to the prayer room and sat down again, trying to

work the thing out. So I had heard or seen or remembered or had presented to me this verse. Then what had happened? (Or was 'then' even the correct word, connoting as it does the passage of time? Because it seemed to me that the event itself had occurred at the same moment that I became aware of the verse of poetry.) Anyway, whenever whatever it was had happened, it had shaken me to my core. I had seemed to see (and yet I had seen nothing) those eyes engraved in the very centre of me. I had seen nothing, and yet I could not have had a more unshakeable conviction that they were there than if I had looked at them then and were still looking at them now. This experience of seeing-but-not-seeing reminded me of something I had once read, and I knew where to find it. This time I started to search through the works of John of the Cross' compatriot, contemporary and friend, Teresa of Avila. This other great Carmelite has written widely on contemplative and mystical prayer and is an authority on the phenomena that sometimes accompany it. Her own life abounded in visions, locutions, ecstasies and raptures, all of which I had found fascinating to read about, in the same detached way that I might have been fascinated to read about the experiences of Neil Armstrong and the other men who first walked on the surface of the moon. Their experiences were thrilling and wonderful, but they bore no resemblance to anything that had ever happened in my own life. Now I was about to consult St Teresa for the first time in relation to what seemed to me to be suspiciously like something she herself might have experienced.

Somewhat cautiously, I thumbed through the various volumes of her writings and at last I found what I was looking for. In her autobiography, known simply as *The Life of St Teresa*, (they weren't into fancy titles for memoirs in the sixteenth century), she attempts to describe an experience that she once had. She suddenly became aware that Jesus was beside her, but she saw nothing. Alarmed by this 'seeing without seeing' she consulted a priest, one of the 'learned men' by whose counsel she put such store. He didn't know what she was talking about. He asked her how she knew it was Jesus. What did he look like? What was he wearing? Teresa couldn't answer any of his questions, and came away even more disturbed than before. Finally, a fortuitous meeting with St Peter of Alcantara – how full of saints Spain was in those days! – put things right. Peter told her that this was one of the highest kinds of vision it was possible to have, and, she adds herself, the one in which the devil can interfere least. In her book *The Interior Castle* she refers again to this experience, explaining that she has since learned that it is called an intellectual vision. In the *Life* she struggles to describe it.

If someone I had never seen or heard about were to come and speak to me when I was blind or in thick darkness and were to tell me who he was, I should believe him, but I should not be able to affirm that he was that person as positively as if I had seen him. But here one can, for though He is unseen He imprints so clear a knowledge on the soul that there seems to be no possibility of doubt. The Lord is pleased to engrave it so deeply on the understanding that one can no more doubt it than one can doubt the evidence of one's eyes. In fact it is easier to doubt one's eyes. For sometimes we wonder whether we have not imagined something seen, whereas here, though that suspicion may arise momentarily, so great a certainty remains behind that the doubt has no validity.

This certainly bore a strong resemblance to what I had just experienced. I hadn't seen any eyes – I couldn't have described their colour, or the expression in them – but I was absolutely certain that they were there, engraved on the deepest part of me. But what did it all mean? It was to be another two years before I even began to understand what might have happened that morning, and in the meantime, the year 2000 had other events in store.

CHAPTER THIRTEEN

Withdraw them, Beloved, for I fly away.
Return thou, dove,
For the wounded hart appears on the hill
At the air of thy flight, and takes refreshment.

For some time following the crystalline fount experience, I half expected it to happen again. Settling down to prayer, I would recall it with a secret inner happiness. But it didn't return, and it became more and more difficult to recapture the experience. Indeed, as time went on, I realised that I had never, even immediately afterwards, been able to recreate for myself what had occurred. For the first few days, the memory of the intensity of the experience was so strong that I could almost (though never quite) confuse it with the event itself. But as time passed even that memory became weaker , until finally, all I could say with certainty was that it had happened, that I had for a moment known that those 'eyes desired' were engraved in my inmost parts and that I could no more doubt it than I could doubt the fact of my existence.

Months later, during what had by then become a bi-annual visit to Aubépine, I discussed this with Véronique. She listened with interest, particularly when I mentioned St Teresa's account of something similar. The prioress of Aubépine and the mystic of Avila were friends of long standing. When I added that it had never happened since, she smiled.

'Indeed', she said. 'And nothing like it may ever happen to you again. Sometimes God send us these things like a piece of manna in the desert. We have to live on them for the rest of our lives.'

This rather pessimistic view of things discouraged me a bit. I realised I had been half hoping that I was about to enter a wonderland of mystical experience, a sort of fairyland for adults, where visions and revelations would abound and where – let's face it – reality could be avoided from time to time. Véronique, who had lived with me for a year and a half, knew me too well. And in any event, I knew enough about the lives of the great mystics now to know that, far from escaping reality, their mystical experiences more often than not plunged them into it in the most unpleasant ways. Take Teresa again, for example: she lived in constant fear of being denounced to the Spanish Inquisition, a very realistic fear in sixteenth-century Spain. It would be difficult to find anything more unpleasantly real than the Inquisition.

Escaping reality is not what religion and the spiritual life is about, as contemplatives of all the great religions know well. The Buddhist concept of 'returning to the marketplace' after attaining enlightenment recognises that it is neither possible nor desirable to remain on heights too far removed from the earth of which we are all made, and that enlightenment, of whatever sort, is not given to us for our own benefit alone. Like Jesus, we must return from the lonely places where we have met God and go out and feed the hungry multitudes – physically as well as metaphorically. 'Thy kingdom come', we pray in the Lord's Prayer. The kingdom of God comes in this life, and if our prayer is genuine, it will push us always to bring about the coming of that kingdom. Yet the desire to stay on the heights is a very human one. Even the great early figures of the Christian tradition were not immune from it. After Peter had witnessed the transfiguration of Jesus on the mountain, he wanted to stay there. 'Lord,' he cried, 'it is good for us to be here. Let us stay here, and I will build three tabernacles, one for you, one for Moses and one for Elijah.' 'For he didn't know what he was saying,' the evangelist remarks drily.

No, Peter didn't know what he was saying, and neither did he know that a short time later he would see a very different Jesus, one sweating and weeping and shaking with terror in Gethsemane. He didn't know that he himself would stand outside the palace of the Jewish High Priest on the most terrible night in human history and deny that he had anything to do with Jesus, or that he had ever known him. He didn't know that he would watch helplessly as Jesus was dragged like a common malefactor through the streets of Jerusalem and then publicly executed in the most ignominious, painful and humiliating way. He didn't know that he would hear that same Jesus who had stood transfigured in majesty on the mountain cry out at the moment of his death to God, his father, asking him why he had abandoned him. This is spirituality at its most earthy.

The vision on the mountain didn't protect Peter from any of the horrors that were to come. If it had, if he had never had to live through the death of Jesus, Peter would never have known the greatest experience of his life, Jesus' resurrection. Our lives on earth are a mixture of pain and of glory, of the deeply earthly and finite experience of being human, and of intimations of immortality.

Easter came and went. I spent the final days of Holy Week, as I had spent them for the previous two years, at Avila, the retreat house of the Carmelite Friars in Donnybrook, Dublin. The friars at that time ran a three-day residential retreat starting on the evening of Holy Thursday and ending after Mass on Easter Sunday. The retreat – which sadly no longer exists, as the residential retreat house has been closed down – was an opportunity to enter in a very total way into the mysteries that were being celebrated. That year, it was also a breathing space for me in the middle of the last stages of the legal formalities and general physical upheaval attendant upon buying and moving into a new house.

The date fixed for the move was at the end of April. After my return from Avila, I was immediately plunged into the business of clearing out the apartment at Mariners Court and buying necessary items for the new house – things I had never owned, either because they were always part of rented accommodation, such as a cooker and a fridge, or because they had never been needed in apartment living, such as a lawnmower and other garden tools. As the days passed, I felt the wrench of leaving Mariners Court more strongly. This was strange. I had moved around a lot in my life, and had never before become attached to a particular flat. This may have been due to the fact that each move I made (leaving out the move to Aubépine, which was of an entirely different order) was to slightly upgraded accommodation, whereas the move I was now making was not. I was upgrading my status from tenant to property-owner, it is true, but in terms both of the accommodation itself and its location, I was going backwards. The new house had none of the airy spaciousness of the Mariners Court apartment. The rooms were cramped and pokey and the kitchen was particularly bleak, looking out on nothing more inspiring than a brick wall in need of whitewashing. The only good things about it were that it had a garden and, like Mariners Court, a second bedroom which I could turn into a prayer room. I already had plans for the garden, which had a glorious view of the Dublin hills. At the moment it was just a long grassy rectangle with a high grey wall at the end, against which some Leylandii were growing and were already about three feet high. Some day they would cover that rather ugly wall, I knew. At each side, the garden was bounded by a low wooden fence. I thought I might plant shrubs along each side, creating a screen of privacy and, by curving the shrubbery out into the lawn, make a sort of little 'room' at the bottom of the garden. There I could put a table and chairs, and on fine days entertain in the garden, because there certainly wasn't going to be much room for doing so in the house itself.

Meanwhile, the ongoing Ansbacher investigation was bringing its own stresses with it. To these was now about to be added the daily commute. The team, comprising the three inspectors and back-up staff, was based in Blackrock. It was easy enough for me, a non-driver, to get from Sutton to Blackrock, because the Dart, Dublin's suburban rail service, brought me practically from door to door in thirty minutes. It would be another matter when I lived in Firhouse; I would first have to get a bus into town, and then catch the Dart from the city centre, thus at least doubling the length of the journey.

In addition to all of this, I was now well into the year of my probation for making a commitment to a life of consecrated celibacy. No decision had yet been made about a date, although Father Hogan had said early on that in view of the fact that I had made a private commitment six years previously, he saw in principle no reason why I shouldn't make a formal commitment at the end of the year. In the meantime, I continued to meet the members of the discernment group at regular intervals. It and my regular meetings with Finbarr at Manresa were my lifelines during a period of rapid change in my life.

Sometimes I looked back in total astonishment at how completely things had changed externally since I had returned to Ireland in 1997 without either a job or a home, and having no idea which direction I should go in my spiritual life. Now the path before me opened up as I needed it. I was never able to see too far ahead, but that didn't matter. When I came, as I occasionally did, to a crossroads without a signpost, Finbarr was there to help me decide which road to take. That, after all, is the purpose of a spiritual director: he or she is an *anam-chara*, a soul friend to accompany one on one's journey. The concept of what spiritual direction is has changed considerably in recent times; indeed, the term 'spiritual accompaniment' is quite often used now instead, and I think it expresses more happily the relationship between director and directee, for a spiritual direction session is an attempt by two people to see where God is at work in the life of one of them. The relationship is necessarily one of great trust on both sides, but especially on the side of the directee, who shares deeply personal experiences with the director. Ironically, it is not the role of the director to be directive (although directors in earlier times believed it was!); instead, the director, by listening to the directee's account of her experience in and outside of prayer, helps her to pay attention to subtle reactions which indicate attraction or resistance to a particular path.

More and more I was realising that God leads those who trust him, who don't try to control the outcome.

CHAPTER FOURTEEN

My Beloved, the mountains,
The solitary, wooded valleys,
The strange islands, the sonorous rivers,
The whisper of the amorous breezes.

Finally the day arrived on which I had to leave Mariners Court. Eileen and Aiden and Kay and her partner Brendan came to help with the move. As the removal men took out the last of the furniture and I whisked around the empty apartment with the vacuum cleaner, the electricity went off, and suddenly I was back in Luxembourg on the evening I left it to join the nuns of Aubépine. I recalled the panic which had suddenly descended on me in the January gloom as I looked around the cold, empty apartment, balcony desolate in the grey half light, and wondered why I was doing this. And then, from nowhere, had come the words of my old friend and mentor, John of the Cross:

On a dark night, kindled in love with yearnings,

Oh, happy chance!

I set forth without being observed,

My house being now at rest.

Those words had cheered me then, redolent as they were of all the nobility of the great quest. Yes, I was leaving a place I loved for the unknown, but what an unknown! I had been sure that there I would find the secret place that John of the Cross spoke of, the place where the Beloved lay sleeping, the place where none appeared …

But the leaving of Mariners Court had none of that nobility and high greatness about it. I was leaving for purely mercenary reasons; leaving a place I loved to go to a place I didn't particularly like, just so that I could own a house and have security in my old age.

I wonder if we ever cease to fool ourselves, to think that the only noble things are those that feel noble. What did I think I was doing in leaving Mariners Court if not beginning another stage of the quest? Had I learned nothing from the experience of leaving Aubépine, which should have taught me that the only way to make progress is to throw away the homemade map and follow the light that shines in our heart? For, as John of the Cross said, describing his own experience:

That light guided me
More surely than the light of noonday
To the place where he (well I knew who!)
Awaited me.

As I now know, it has led me to the little house in Firhouse as surely as it had led me everywhere else up to that time; as I know it will lead me always. Because that burning light, as John explains, is the light of faith. That faith is at the same time fire and water, a flame and a fountain, hiding in its depths the eyes desired which are outlined in our inmost parts. It is those beloved eyes that see the way ahead.

But I wasn't able to I see any of that during the first months in Firhouse. Even though I knew the area well, it seemed to me in my then state of mind an alien place. I didn't know anybody. Although this had never worried me in any of my previous moves, here I felt terribly insecure. Part of it was the fact of living in a house after so many years of apartment living. I had never felt alone or insecure in any apartment I had lived in. If I heard a strange noise in the night, I assumed it was coming from someone else's apartment, and didn't worry about it. But now, the least sound at night had me jerking into instant wakefulness. Was it inside the house? If so, it could only be a burglar! I slept very badly for a long time. The journey to the office every day was, in spite of its length, a relief. Little by little, as the bus approached the city, I felt myself returning to familiar territory. Reaching the office, I felt I was back in civilisation again. I dreaded the return journey in the evening, and the sight of my own hall door was like the sight of a prison.

I've never really worked out why the move to Firhouse proved to be so traumatic. Perhaps the experience of once again

leaving somewhere that I wanted to stay had revived unre-
solved issues from the leaving of Aubépine. I only know that the
trauma continued for two months, and then passed. From then
on, Firhouse has been home.

In spite of – or perhaps because of – the way I was feeling, I
was anxious from the beginning to get involved in parish activi-
ties. I liked the look of Firhouse parish church. It was a bright
and airy building, about thirty years old, with gardens on each
side visible from the huge picture windows. The local community
appeared to be very committed to the parish. With this in mind,
I approached the priest after Mass a few Sundays after I had
moved in. He asked me where I was living.

'But you're not in this parish at all,' he said, when I told him.
'Although your postal address is Firhouse, where you are living
is in the parish of Bohernabreena.'

I was bitterly disappointed. The parish church of Firhouse
was very near the Carmelite monastery, and gave me a sense of
being on home ground that I lacked for the rest of the time. The
priest said he would tell the local curate that there was someone
new in his parish and ask him to call. A couple of evenings later,
while I was preparing dinner, the door bell rang. A youngish
man with an engaging grin was standing on the doorstep. He introduced himself as the Bohernabreena curate, Father Hugh
Kavanagh, and he explained that he was responsible for the part
of the parish I was living in.

The parish of Bohernabreena is an unusual one, in that it is
divided into two quite distinct parts. Bohernabreena itself and St
Anne's, its beautiful old stone parish church, is located high in
the Dublin hills. I had often visited it with my father in our ram-
bles through the hills when I was a child. When we passed it, my
father would insist on calling in to say a prayer, churches in
those relatively crime-free days being open all day.

The area had another memory for me too. It was near
Bohernabreena, in a place called Piperstown, that at the age of
sixteen I had what I can only describe as a mystical experience.
My father and I had been walking all afternoon in the hills, and

as evening drew near, we were making our way back towards
Bohernabreena. At Piperstown, we crossed the crest of the hill
and began a descent into a valley. It was a still, sultry afternoon
in late summer. We had been chatting in a desultory fashion, but
now we fell silent, both tired after the long hike. We reached the
valley floor. I looked up, and saw that we were surrounded on
all sides by the purple and black hills, which in their towering
height seemed to close out even the sky. A brooding sense of
presence hung over the place and I felt everything inside me
hush. I forgot my father was with me; I forgot I was there myself.
For a moment, the presence that filled the valley excluded every
other form of being.

When we reached home, in a desperate attempt to somehow
capture what had happened, I went to my bedroom and took
down the copybook in which I had begun to write what I like to
think was poetry, and penned the following:

I stood amid the cloisters of the hills
and was at peace.
To me the gleaming rills
were as some sweet-voiced choir of nuns
who pray for lesser souls
and ever day by day grow nearer God.
And I was then at peace
and near him, and I knew he would not cease
to love me.
'Yes, my soul's employ will hence be for my God', I gladly
vowed.
The hills lay wrappèd in an evening cloud
and dreamed. And as night fell I lingered still,
Alone, enraptured, 'neath the holy hill.

Awful stuff, of course, full of adolescent romantic dreaming and
of the notion that nuns are better than other people. And not
even accurate; I hadn't after all, lingered there alone as night fell.
I had gone home with my father well before dark. Yet even
today it captures for me something of the truth of what had oc-

curred that evening, of that terrible yet peaceful brooding Presence that I knew loved me,

So in returning to Bohernabreena, I was returning in a sense to my spiritual roots. But the part of the parish I was based in was not in the hills, for Bohernabreena had grown considerably since I was sixteen. St Anne's now had, I discovered, a chapel of ease, a little prefabricated building called Holy Rosary Church, in an area called Ballycragh, downhill from the parish church itself, and within ten minutes walk from where I lived. Holy Rosary was presided over by Father Hugh, while St Anne's was the domain of the parish priest.

I liked Father Hugh at once, as did everyone who met him. He had an onerous task in building a community around Holy Rosary Church, as the area was a developing one, populated mainly by young families. Many of these either didn't attend church at all, or returned for Sunday worship to the churches of their places of origin. But once people had met Hugh, they tended to go to Holy Rosary, and when they went once, they came back again. Hugh had a homely way with him that people responded to and he was particularly successful with children and young people who liked his practical, no-nonsense spirituality.

It was to be in that little pre-fabricated church that I would make my public commitment to God, and it was to be in that parish that I would meet some people who would become not only friends, but a sort of spiritual community. But I knew none of that yet.

CHAPTER FIFTEEN

The tranquil night,
At the time of the rising of the dawn,
The silent music, the sounding solitude,
The supper that recreates and enkindles love.

There was only one Mass on Sundays in Holy Rosary Church, the other parish Mass taking place in St Anne's. I joined the choir that sang at the Sunday morning Mass. There was, however, a vigil Mass on Saturday evenings, and sometimes I went to that as well. The choir didn't sing at that Mass; instead there was a cantor, a girl with a beautiful soprano voice that I loved listening to. She was often accompanied on the guitar by another young woman. I never saw either of them at any other time, and I wondered if they lived in the parish or were just visiting. I liked the look of them and thought I would like to get to know them.

Meantime, the year of discernment planned by Fr Martin Hogan was drawing to a close. I had met throughout the year individually and collectively with the members of the group that he had set up, and with Finbarr, and we were all in agreement that it seemed right for me to make a commitment to a life of consecrated celibacy. The next question to be decided was where the ceremony should take place. Liturgically, it is a community event, and ideally should take place in the local church of the person to be consecrated. But many people prefer a more private ceremony, often in a church or oratory belonging to a religious order or congregation with which they have some particular affinity. Father Hugh, enthusiastic at the idea of such an event taking place in his parish, tried to encourage me to hold the ceremony in Holy Rosary Church. But shrinking from anything so public, my own first idea was to ask the nuns of Firhouse Carmel if I could have it in their chapel, a place that held many memories for me. This turned out to be impractical, because the community was at that time beginning major building work on their monastery, work that involved the complete demolition of the existing buildings including the chapel, and the construction of new ones on the same site.

So it was by default that I returned reluctantly to Father Hugh, who, of course, was delighted. I explained that I would like to have the ceremony quietly, at a private Mass.

'Oh, that would be a pity.' said Hugh. 'This is something that should take place in the heart of the community. My own idea would be to have it take place during Sunday Mass.'

I was at first horrified by this idea, but said I would think about it. Finally, without feeling any happier at the idea of making such an exhibition of myself – how would I explain to people what I was doing? How would I explain that this was not the same thing as becoming a nun? – I recognised that Hugh was right. It was an event that belonged in the heart of the local church.

Hugh was full of ideas. He decided that it would be a good idea to have a second Sunday Mass on that day, and to hold the ceremony during it, so that the parishioners wouldn't feel obliged to be present at it if they didn't want to be. He offered to help me with the preparation of the leaflets for the Mass, once I had chosen the readings, and I accepted gratefully. He was expert on the computer; I wasn't.

The rite of consecration of virgins, as it is called, is performed by a bishop – generally the local bishop. Our local bishop was Bishop Eamonn Walsh. He was an unassuming man, one who didn't stand too much on ceremony. He was pleased that I was going to make the commitment at a Sunday Mass. The only problem for him, he explained, when we met to discuss matters in a coffee shop near my office, was that he had only one Sunday free over the following months. That Sunday was the 15 October.

Delighted, I explained that it was the very date I would have chosen myself. The 15 October is the feast day of St Teresa of Avila, the great Carmelite mystic and friend of St John of the Cross. The fact that it fell on a Sunday that year, and that it was the only Sunday the bishop was free, seemed to me to be highly significant. It was as though St Teresa was giving the whole venture the mark of her approval. I remembered a dream that had greatly impressed me when I was in Aubépine. I was dancing down a staircase at an exhilarating speed, hand in hand with St Teresa. I knew that she was dancing in this exuberant way because of her great love for God. And I knew that I was dancing only because she was holding my hand.

Once the date for the ceremony was set, all that remained to be done was to arrange the liturgy and send out the invitations. I wanted to have music at the Mass. Hugh suggested asking the parish choir to sing, and I liked that idea. Then I thought of the two young women who sang and played at the Saturday evening Mass. I thought it would be nice if they did one or two solos during the ceremony. In particular, there was a song of Liam Lawton's that I had heard them do once or twice – *The Hiding Place* – that seemed particularly appropriate. Hugh agreed, so I decided to ask them after evening Mass the following Saturday. Hugh had told me their names: Áine Mulvey was the singer and Mairéad Flanagan the guitarist. I approached them a bit diffidently the following Saturday, and explained what I was about to do. They were friendly and interested and to my delight, agreed to take part.

The ceremony involves the giving of a ring to the woman making the commitment. This ring is the only outward symbol that the woman wears. I had been wearing a ring since the day in 1994 that I had made a private vow of celibacy, but I wanted something special for this occasion. After much searching, I found, in a small jewellers in Wicklow Street, a gold ring embossed with the design that runs around the rim of the Ardagh Chalice, an ancient gold chalice preserved in the National Museum of Ireland. It was perfect, with its double symbolism of Eucharist and nationality. I bought it.

On the day of the ceremony everything went well. Many parishioners came, and to my own surprise, I wasn't embarrassed at all. The choir was in great voice, and Áine's rendition of *The Hiding Place*, accompanied by Mairéad, was exactly what I had wanted. Afterwards, family and friends came back to the little house in Firhouse for lunch, and when they had all gone home, Irene and I sat down together quietly for a while. I felt peacefully content. Another step had been taken and it felt very right.

The ceremony had an unexpected outcome. Mairéad Flanagan became a close friend. Later that year, she and I and another friend, Maeve Kerney, began a small prayer group which met in my house once a fortnight. From a small beginning it has grown over the years, and now has a permanent core of eight members, all living in the neighbourhood.

We continue to meet once a fortnight, taking it in turn to prepare the prayer for the week. Once a year, we go away for a day of prayer and reflection together. It is a huge support for me to be able to spend time with like-minded friends. One evening, Finbarr came to say Mass in the house for us. It was the first time he had met the other members of the group. Afterwards he remarked to me how lucky I was to have come to know such people. He didn't need to tell me. I already knew.

Meanwhile, the Ansbacher investigation was dragging on. It seemed to have taken on a life of its own, and sometimes I wondered whether it would ever end. At the beginning of September 2001, it entered its third year. A few days later I went out during the lunch break to get a manicure at the nearby Blackrock Shopping Centre. The salon was full of noise and activity, the radio providing a constant background noise that nobody was paying any attention to. As I was paying my bill, the news came on. It was the tone of the newsreader's voice that caught my attention: it sounded unusually excited. I tried to listen to what he was saying above the din of voices in the salon. There was something about a number of people dead in New York.

'What is he saying, can you hear it?' I asked the girl at the desk.

'I think there was a plane crash in New York,' she said.

I went back to the office and into the kitchen where we kept a small radio. I switched it on and it burst into that appalling scream that was to be replayed over and over during the weeks of horror that followed:

'People are jumping, oh my God, people are jumping!'

It was 9/11.

CHAPTER SIXTEEN

Drive us away the foxes,
For our vineyard is now in flower,
While we make a bunch of roses,
And let none appear upon the hill.

In January 2002 I went to Manresa to make an eight-day directed retreat – something that had become an annual event since the three days in January of 1998 when all the pain and bitterness of the leaving of Aubépine had disappeared forever. This retreat began unusually peacefully. From the moment of my arrival I sank into a silence and calm that was not, for me, habitual at the start of a retreat. Normally I arrive toting all the inner luggage of the previous year, and the first couple of days are spent in gradually dumping it. But this was different. As I stood at the window of my room that night before going to bed, looking out at the shadowy garden and beyond at the lights encircling Dublin Bay, the deep peace which enfolded me suddenly reminded me of the morning of the crystal fountain, as I had begun to privately call it. It was a while since I had thought about it, but now it began to exercise a strange fascination over my mind. I had never satisfactorily explained to myself what it was that had happened that morning. It was difficult now to recapture how I had felt and what I had experienced, but I was as certain as I had been then that I had known that the eyes of the Beloved were engraved on my inmost parts.

Next day, when I met Finbarr for one of his chats, I told him what was on my mind. Of course I had told him about it at the time, but now he was more interested in why it had suddenly begun to preoccupy me, so long after the event.

'Why don't you ask God if there's something he wants to tell you about that experience,' he suggested, 'and then try to remain open to whatever it is.'

In my room later that day I reflected again upon the verse, and suddenly the obvious hit me. I could not understand why I had never seen it before. Now it was perfectly clear. The verse was a request, a prayer: 'if on that thy silvered surface thou wouldst of a sudden form the eyes desired'. It was like the prayer of Moses: 'Lord, let me see your face!' It was a prayer that, on that morning in 2000, I had no intention of making, nor indeed had I realised until this moment that of course that was what I had done. I had prayed to see the 'eyes desired'. Why had I made that prayer? I didn't know. It had come from no conscious volition of mine; it seemed rather to have been presented to me. Then I remembered what St Paul had told the Romans:

> Likewise the Spirit helps us in our weakness; for we do not know how to pray as we ought, but that very Spirit intercedes with sighs too deep for words. And God, who searches the heart, knows what is the mind of the Spirit, because the Spirit intercedes for the saints according to the will of God. (Romans 8:26-27)

The Spirit, then, had made that prayer for me, and now I understood what had happened. The prayer of the Spirit, because it had been in accordance with the mind of God, had been answered immediately. I had seen the desired eyes. For a moment, the silver surface of the crystal fountain had broken, and I had seen what it concealed. What I had always believed – that God lives in us – I had, for a moment, known.

The next morning, I reported my findings to Finbarr. He picked up a book that had been lying on the table beside him.

'I had a look at St John of the Cross myself last night', he remarked. 'Have you read his analysis of that verse?'

If I had, I couldn't remember anything in particular about it.

'What does he say?' I asked, curious.

Finbarr handed me the book. I looked first at the annotation which preceded the stanza.

> At this season, (John begins) the soul feels within itself such a vehement desire to journey to God that it is like a stone that is approaching ever nearer to its centre. Or, again, it feels like the wax that has begun to receive the impression of the seal and has not perfectly received its form ...

He continues in this vein for a little and then concludes

> It knows not what to do save to turn to faith itself, as to that
> which encloses and conceals within itself the form and beauty
> of its Beloved, from which it likewise receives the [...] shad-
> ows and pledges of love. The soul then speaks to faith ...

Yes, there was confirmation of what had just dawned on me: 'it
knows not what to do' – echoes there of 'we do not know how to
pray as we ought'. Powerlessness is fertile ground for the Spirit,
because the Spirit meets no resistance there. The only thing that
stops God working wonders in our lives is our own perpetual
desire to be in control. I put the book down for a moment.
Something else had struck me.

'You know,' I remarked, 'John of the Cross can be very mis-
leading. His language is so beautiful and so grandiose that you
are inclined to think that the experiences he describes are terribly exalted and rarefied, things ordinary people couldn't possibly aspire too. But in fact, when you start to examine the reality
of what he is saying, you suddenly realise that it fits some experience of your own.'

It reminded me of when I had read his metaphor of the wood
and the fire while I was in Aubépine. It had happened at a time
when I seemed to be going from bad to worse, losing my temper
in public and generally being unable to maintain even the façade
of a mature forty-something. During a community retreat we
had at that time, the retreat director, a Jesuit priest, had remarked that God's love was like a fire. Struck by this, I began to
apply it to the various things that were happening in my life
and, remembering that John of the Cross had made a similar
comparison in the *Dark Night of the Soul*, I had looked it up.
There he compares the action of God upon the person trying to
surrender to him with the action of fire upon wood.

> [The fire] makes it black, dark and unsightly, and even to
> give forth a bad odour...

says John, and with a sudden shock I had realised that he wasn't
talking about some profound inner experience whereby this
seemed to be happening, while outwardly the person grew daily

in sanctity and in the estimation of all (two concepts which I was finding it difficult to separate). No, he was stating a fact: the person's façade begins to break down, real faults begin to emerge, and everyone notices, just as they would notice the bad smell from the wood. Everyone begins to see just how imperfect this person is.

I could laugh at this now; I hadn't laughed too hard then.

'Anyway,' said Finbarr, pulling me back to the present, 'what is it about the crystal fountain experience that makes you say that?'

'Well,' I said, 'that morning was just like any other morning. It took some effort to get up that bit early in order to have time for prayer. I didn't feel very prayerful. I began in a very distracted sort of way, with things on my mind that had nothing to do with God.'

'But you were there, all the same,' said Finbarr. 'You went to the meeting place. No one was forcing you. No one was going to check up later to see whether you had gone or not.'

'True,' I said, 'But does a person dragging themselves unwillingly out of bed and then sitting down to prayer in a distracted sort of way sound to you like a soul that "feels within itself such a vehement desire to journey to God that it is like a stone that is approaching ever nearer to its centre"?'

He laughed.

'I see your point. Anyone reading that passage would expect that such a person would leap out of bed all on fire with this desire, rush to the prayer room and be immediately lost in prayer. And yet, it was of course that vehement desire, which you nevertheless didn't *feel* at all on any conscious level, which got you out of bed that morning.'

'Yes,' I said. 'And then the next thing that happened was exactly what he describes, but it didn't happen at all in the way you would expect. I tried to let go, to hand it over, to stop controlling, to trust that there was someone else present who had an interest in the prayer taking place. Isn't that really the sort of thing John of the Cross is talking about when he says "It [the soul] knows not what to do save to turn to faith itself"? That actually means nothing more than that the person believes that God is there. And it's true: I didn't know what else to do!'

'You know,' I went on, 'I don't think most people realise that mystical experience doesn't necessarily mean conscious experience. I certainly didn't for a long time. Yet extraordinary things can be taking place between oneself and God while all one is conscious of is the fact that one has a bad itch, or that the windows need washing.'

Thoughtfully, I picked up the book again, turning this time to John's explanation of the verse itself. His analysis was typically dry and scholarly:

She calls faith 'crystalline' for two reasons: the first, because it is from Christ her spouse, and the second, because it has the properties of crystal in being pure in its truths, and strong, and clear and free from errors and natural forms ...

All very interesting, no doubt, but not particularly enlightening. I looked up at Finbarr queryingly.

'Try the following stanza,' he suggested.

I looked at it.

'Withdraw them, Beloved, for I fly away' it began. Withdraw what? Oh, the desired eyes, of course! This stanza indicates that the request made in the previous one has somehow been granted. Eagerly I read on.

As the soul has just now desired those Divine eyes with such great yearning, even as she has just said in the foregoing stanza, the Beloved has revealed to her some rays of his greatness and divinity, as she has desired.

I stopped and went back again, reading more carefully.

'Finbarr', I said, 'am I understanding this properly? If you take the verses that begin with the crystalline fount one, you have the following scenario. The person seeking God asks faith to show her the eyes which she has desired to see, and which by faith she knows are engraved in her inmost heart. That's the 'crystalline fount' verse. The next verse begins 'Withdraw them,

Beloved, for I fly away.' That means, according to John, that the prayer made in the previous verse has been granted, and that the person is so overwhelmed by the vision of the eyes that she asks the Beloved to withdraw them – they are making her 'fly away'

I stopped doubtfully.

'I never felt at any stage that I was flying away', I said. 'And just look at what John says about that; it has even less application to me. He says:

> That we may the better understand what flight is this, it is to be noted that, as we have said, in that visitation of the Divine Spirit the spirit of the soul is enraptured with great force, to commune with the Spirit [...] And it is for this reason that in these raptures and flights the body remains without its senses, and, although the greatest pains be inflicted upon it, it feels them not ...

I laughed. No, that certainly wasn't me. Here was another example of how dangerous it was to take St John of the Cross too literally. Not everyone has the temperament of the sixteenth-century mystics, given as they were to raptures and ecstasy. But that doesn't mean that the rest of us rather unecstatic people of the twenty-first century cannot have the authentic underlying experience that gave rise to those raptures.

Ruth Burrows explains all this very well in her book *Guidelines for Mystical Prayer*. She distinguishes between what she calls 'light on' and 'light off' contemplation; the 'light on' kind being that where the contemplative can, as it were, 'see', what is happening, usually because their prayer is accompanied by mystical phenomena, whereas the 'light off' person has the same contemplative and mystical experience, but without being able to see what is happening. It rarely reflects itself in sensible experience. St John of the Cross and St Teresa of Avila were 'light on' mystics; St Thérèse of Lisieux was 'light off'.

'Light off' has her own deep wisdom communicated direct from divine wisdom but, as Thérèse says, she finds it within her without knowing where it has come from. It seems like her own wisdom, flowing as it does through natural aqueducts. It is as truly God's wisdom as is that of visions, but in the latter case the subject of them is aware that God is here and now drawing her attention to what he would reveal to her. 'Light off' carries its own depth of certainty, and yet perhaps in God's loving care for his children he knows that in our darkness and obscurity we need from time to time a flash of lightning to show us the truth of our truth, the certainty of what we know is certain. (Burrows, *Guidelines for Mystical Prayer*).

'Well,' said Finbarr now, 'forget about the "flying away" bit, and concentrate on what John says has actually happened.'

I read the passage again. This time it leaped out at me: 'the Beloved has revealed to her some rays of his greatness and divinity'. This is what the 'vision' of the eyes was: a ray of the greatness and divinity of God. For the moment, I couldn't think beyond that extraordinary fact.

But we are living on earth, not in heaven, so at the end of this momentous retreat, I had to go back to work, where at last we were nearing the end of the Ansbacher investigation. It was time to begin the onerous task of preparing our report – a report that, as we could see already, was going to be voluminous. The investigation had given me much food for thought. We had interviewed almost two hundred people who at some time either had an account in the offshore bank or had known something about the way in which the bank had been organised. After some time, it became apparent to us that not everyone who had opened an account in the Cayman Islands had done so with the intention of evading tax. The line between tax evasion and legitimate tax avoidance is often blurred, and some of the people we interviewed had taken advice in good faith from accountants or other financial experts who had assured them that the scheme was a legitimate one. These people now found themselves summoned to account for themselves before a tribunal which had power to examine them under oath. It was a deeply distressing experience for them. Many of them were old by this time, and some were ill. Others were surviving spouses of deceased account holders who had inherited the account without any understanding of how it had been established. Our terms of reference obliged us to publish the names of all those who had held Ansbacher accounts in the Cayman Islands, so these people faced the prospect of seeing their names appear in the public press in the context of an investigation that had provoked much public interest and outcry. In the end, we published their names, but making it clear that they were unaware of the nature of what they were doing.

But what of the others, those who did indeed know that they were evading tax? Face to face with them as we interviewed them one after the other, I was aware of how easily it could have been me at the other side of the table. We are all very ready to decry such behaviour in others, but given the same opportunity, would we behave any differently? We hope so, but 'what does he know who has not been tried?' The 1970s and early 1980s were periods of heavy taxation in Ireland. In 1974, the top rate of income tax was a crippling 80%. This reduced to 60% at the end of the 1970s and continued at that rate for almost a decade. As Colm Keena says in his book *The Ansbacher Conspiracy* (Gill & Macmillan, 2003):

> These rates created a strong temptation to evade income tax, a temptation which a significant proportion of the non-PAYE population found impossible to resist.

The wealthy were further penalised by a tax of 26% on profits from the purchase and sale of assets introduced in 1974, and by a tax of up to 60% on gifts and inheritances introduced in 1975. To this already onerous financial burden was added, from 1975 to 1978, a wealth tax, a 1% levy on the assets of the rich.

> These taxes created great concern, if not outrage and consternation, among the more well-off sections of society. The new taxes created two impulses: the impulse to seek to have the taxes abolished and the impulse to avoid or evade them. (*The Ansbacher Conspiracy*)

People who had built up wealth by hard work saw much more than half of it going to the government. It was a period of huge financial uncertainty and, given the opportunity of secreting some of their wealth away for their children, some people succumbed. Would I, if I had been rich in the 1970s? It is easy now to say that I would not. This, and similar questions, troubled my mind throughout the investigation. Who was I to judge anyone else?

By the time we had reached the final stages of the investigation, the original team had changed. We had started with three inspectors: Judge Declan Costello, Paul Rowan, a retired partner from PricewaterhouseCooper and me. When Judge Costello was forced to retire midway through on health grounds, Paul and I wondered how we would manage without him. It didn't seem possible that anyone coming fresh to the investigation at that stage, more than a year on, could possibly come to grips with all we had by then discovered. We had reckoned, however, without Sean O'Leary.

Judge Sean O'Leary had been a barrister back in the days when I had been in practice at the Bar, but I hadn't known him, because he practised mainly on the Cork Circuit, while I was based in Dublin. He had become a judge after I had left the Bar to go to work in Luxembourg, which meant that I had never appeared in his court. So it was with some apprehension that I took a phone call from him the day after his appointment to replace Judge Costello. Five minutes later, I felt totally reassured. The affable Cork accent on the other end of the phone could clearly only belong to an equally affable owner, which proved to be indeed the case. Sean O'Leary's arrival at the investigation, while it didn't quite turn it into a party, gave rise nevertheless to many hilarious moments. He turned out to be a talented writer of limericks, and before long, coffee-breaks in the office were enlivened by the recitation of his latest creation.

But if Sean was a good companion, both on the job and socially, it was in his speedy grasp of the entire investigation so far and his ability to focus it into the future that he was at his most impressive. He had a talent for grasping an issue in its totality and identifying precisely what needed to be done to address it. Nothing was too difficult, and he was scathing of those who made mountains out of molehills. 'Ah yes,' he would say of such persons, 'there's no solution without a problem!'

By the time Judge Costello retired and Sean took his place, it had dawned on all of us that the investigation was bigger than anyone had at first suspected. For that reason, the government decided to seek the appointment of an additional inspector who would work part-time. This was Michael Cush, Senior Counsel. He was, however, a familiar friend, as he had been up to that time legal adviser to the inspectorate. My own connection with him went back much further. We had been in the same year in Kings Inns, he, a young student fresh from college, I a thirty-four year old attempting to qualify as a barrister after having spent eleven years, from the age of eighteen, in a Carmelite monastery.

Our class in Kings Inns was a mixed one age-wise, as classes in Kings Inns always are. The majority of the class were young law graduates, but it was also possible to do the Bar exams without out a law degree, by acquiring Kings Inns' own Diploma in Legal Studies. In my year the holders of this diploma varied in age from mid twenties to over seventy. This disparate group of which I was a member was known to the young law graduates as 'the Wrinklies' much to my fury, who neither felt, nor looked, in the least wrinkly. A couple of weeks after the year commenced, an article appeared in the students' magazine. It contained a number of unflattering comments about the Wrinklies as a group, and it was signed 'Michael Cush'. I was enraged. Our year was a particularly large one, and I didn't know this Michael Cush, but he was certainly going to hear from me when I finally identified him.

A few days later, my friends and I were having one of the many dinners in Kings Inns that the rules obliged us to eat in order to be called to the Bar. We had booked a table for eight people, but one of our group hadn't shown up. Accordingly, when, just before grace, a lone late student arrived at the door of the Dining Hall and looked around somewhat desperately for somewhere to seat himself, we beckoned him over to our table. He sat down and joined immediately in the conversation that was already going on, and between one thing and another, we didn't get around to introducing ourselves until about half-way through the meal, when it occurred to somebody that we didn't know his name. 'Michael Cush,' he said, in answer to our query.

'What!' I leaped to my feet, infuriated. 'Are you the person who called me a Wrinkly?'

'Oh no,' he groaned, 'not that article again!'

It appeared I had not been the first person to attack him about it.

Anyway, here was Michael now many years later, as well qualified as any of us to be numbered among the ranks of the Wrinklies. He was a valuable addition to the team, both in terms of his analytical skills, his massive store of legal knowledge and the quiet good humour and total reasonableness with which he always managed to defuse the occasional tensions that arose.

In this group of legal inspectors, Paul Rowan was the odd man out, being neither a judge nor a barrister. Paul was an accountant, and if it wasn't for him, much of the complexities of the scheme we were investigating would have passed over the heads of the rest of us. However, he found an ally in Sean, who had also been an accountant before giving it up to take up the law. Bon vivant, entrepreneur and total gentleman in the best sense of the term, Paul became a friend as well as a colleague – a friendship that endures to this day.

The end of the investigation meant different things for each of us. For Sean, the investigation had been simply a hiatus in his life as a judge, to which he would return when it was over. For Michael Cush, because he was only a part-time inspector, it simply meant that he could devote his full attention once more to his legal practice. For Paul, it meant that he could at last take up the various interests with which he hoped to fill his retirement. But for me, it meant that I would have to start a new job. The reader will recall that I had just resigned from the Competition Authority and was about to take up a new job in the Attorney General's office at the time the investigation had started. This job had been put on hold in the intervening years, but it was now almost time to take it up. While I was looking forward to it in one way, in another, I didn't relish the prospect of yet another change. My life, there was no doubt about it, had been pretty *mouvementé* to date, as the French would say. But it was now about to go around in a complete circle.

CHAPTER SEVENTEEN

Stay thee, dead north wind.
Come, south wind, that awakenest love;
Breathe through my garden and let its odours flow,
And the Beloved shall pasture among the flowers.

One Friday, I opened the business section of the *Irish Times*, and there, with a sense of deja-vu, my eye was caught, just as it had been in Luxembourg five years earlier, by the heading 'Legal Adviser'. The Competition Authority was once more looking for a legal advisor. This time, however, it was offered as a permanent position, at a higher grade than formerly. Because this addressed the reasons why I had left three years earlier, I now decided to re-apply.

There is a terrible risk involved in applying for a job that you have already held. If you don't succeed, what does that say about the way you carried out your duties in the past? It was, then, a very nervous me who learned that I had been short-listed for interview. I took a few hours off from the Ansbacher investigation on a raw March morning and attended at the offices of the Civil Service and Local Appointments Commission. There were four people on the interview panel, one of them being the recently appointed new chairman of the Competition Authority, Dr John Fingleton. I had never worked with John Fingleton, but I had heard that he had made a number of changes to the way the Authority was run since taking over the year before. He had also increased staff numbers, so that the Authority had grown considerably since I had been there before. I had met him once, at a reception to mark the tenth anniversary of the creation of the Competition Authority, and had been struck by his energy and friendly informality.

I never really know how to rate my own performance at job interviews. Does anyone? Even if you feel you've done fairly well, you have no idea who you are competing against or how well they have done. This interview seemed to go off reasonably well; at least I didn't feel I had made a fool of myself. I had explained to the panel, however, that should I be successful, I wouldn't be able to take up the position until we had completed the Ansbacher report, an event which we anticipated would take place around June.

Standing on the bleak Dart platform waiting for a train back to Blackrock, I told myself that I might as well put it out of my head for the moment; the Civil Service and Local Appointments Commission was known, like the mills of God, to grind slowly, and one could not expect to hear anything from them for at least a month after an interview, and usually much longer.

The following morning, when I arrived at the office as usual at nine o'clock, there was a message from John Fingleton, asking me to ring him. I froze. John Fingleton could only have one reason for ringing me: I must have failed, but, knowing that I had held the position before, he, out of kindness, wanted to tell me so himself, rather than have me hear it from the official source in a more impersonal way.

I went into my office and closed the door. Taking a deep breath, I picked up the phone and dialled the number. John's energetic voice answered immediately. He wasted no time in getting to the point: he was ringing, he said, to let me know that I had got the job, and he knew I was unlikely to hear this officially for weeks. In the meantime, he would like to meet me as soon as possible to discuss a number of matters. How would Saturday afternoon suit?

It suited fine. This was my first experience of John Fingleton's enthusiastic attitude to everything, an attitude that I was to come to know and appreciate over the following years. I was delighted. Now at last, instead of having to make yet another change, I would be returning to something familiar, to a place where I had enjoyed working. In the meantime, the team and I got on with writing the report. It was published, as planned, in June. Its publication attracted huge attention, with ordinary members of the public queuing up outside the Government

Publications Office on the Saturday it was published, to buy their copy – or rather, their copies, for it ran to several volumes. That morning I had the rather surreal experience of sitting in the bus on the way to town listening on my Walkman to the Tánaiste publicly thanking me and the other inspectors by name. Such was the public interest that RTÉ was broadcasting live from outside the Government Publications Office and interviewing people as they went in to buy the report. I recall one young mother who went in pushing her toddler in his buggy and came out again holding him by the hand, his place in the buggy having been taken by the volumes of our report. Another episode in the adventure of my life had come to an end.

My life, however, was not yet destined to become quiet and uneventful. The desire to write about Aubépine had never really left me, and throughout 2002 it began to be pressing. I had gradually come to see the Aubépine experience as a highly significant happening in the context of the whole quest, leading as it did to an abandonment to God that, it seemed to me, had paved the way for the crystal fountain experience. I opened up the old files on my computer where I had jotted down disjointed episodes from the year and a half I had spent there. Somehow, I still couldn't see where such a book might begin or end, but from time to time I wrote a few more pages anyway.

In the summer of 2003, one of my colleagues in the Competition Authority told me about a yoga class she had enrolled in at the People's College in Parnell Square, thinking that I might like to join her. Looking at the brochure she had given me, I discovered that the College, which was just across the road from the Competition Authority's offices, had some really interesting classes. Leafing through it, I was idly considering taking up the guitar or the tin whistle, when the words 'creative writing' leaped out at me. Abandoning all thoughts of yoga, I rang Kay, persuaded her that she needed to do a creative writing course and enrolled both of us.

The class took place once a week. Our teacher, Susan Knight, also taught creative writing in University College Dublin. At the end of the first session, she set us some homework for the following week. We were to write a short piece descriptive of some event in our past. I handed in what is now the prologue to *The Secret Ladder*, the nostalgic piece in remembrance of Aubépine that had been inspired by *Brideshead Revisited*. Susan was very encouraging about it, and I began to feel that maybe I had found the right voice in which to write. But the real breakthrough came some weeks later, when Susan explained the classic forms of the novel. Describing the form of the quest story, she told us that traditionally, the hero sets out on a journey in search of something, but when he finally reaches what he thinks is journey's end, he discovers that what he is looking for is not there; he must go further. Suddenly I saw the entire outline of my book. It would begin in Luxembourg, where I first realised there was a quest to be undertaken, and it would end with the leaving of Aubépine and the realisation that what I was seeking was not there, that I would have to go further.

I started the very next day. I made up my mind to do a certain amount, no matter how little, every day. At first, I spent ten or fifteen minutes of my lunch hour at it. Then, as it began to take shape, I spent a couple of hours each weekend. By mid-December, I had written about 15,000 words, and I decided it was time to get someone's opinion as to whether it was worth going on with. With some trepidation, I showed it to my brother Liam, a journalist whose writing I admire greatly and whose opinion I respect. To my astonishment, he was very enthusiastic about what I had written so far and strongly urged me to go ahead.

As it happened, I had planned to spend that Christmas at Aubépine, and I decided to bring my laptop with me and do some serious writing. Writing about Aubépine in Aubépine was a moving experience. Sitting in my room, looking out at the familiar landscape, I lived over again the Sunday of my first visit. It had been a miserably wet day, and I had had no idea how I was going to fill in the time. The visit to this remote monastery in the depths of the French countryside had seemed like one big mistake. Then I had picked up the bible that is provided in every bedroom in the *hôtellerie*, and, opening it at random, I had read the following words:

Arise my love, my fair one, and come away;

For now the winter is past, the rain is over and gone.

Time stopped. The words had seemed addressed to me personally, and they were the impetus that ultimately resulted in my joining the community.

My life had taken some odd twists and turns since that day. I had taken those words from scripture to be an invitation to dedicate my life to God in the monastery of Aubépine. My attempt to do so had seemed in the end to be a disaster. I had thought I had destroyed the quest; that I had gone so far astray that it would be impossible ever to find my way back onto the road. But 'God writes straight with crooked lines' says an old Irish proverb. I now knew that Aubépine was only part – although an essential part – of a journey that was ongoing, of a quest where at every moment the One I was seeking guided my next step.

By the time I returned to Dublin in the New Year, I had completed more than half the book, and had sketched out the outline of the remainder. It was easy to continue during the months that followed. I began to consider the question of publication. Several people had told me that I would get nowhere without an agent. Publishers were not interested in reading unsolicited manuscripts from unknown writers, they said, unless they were sent in by reputable agents.

I didn't know any agents. One evening, I did a Google search for Irish agents. It turned up a small list. There was only one name I recognised, that of a woman whose name had recently been in the press because she had achieved an extraordinary advance on royalties for a first novel. I would ask her to take me on, I thought; in my naiveté believing that you employed a literary agent in the same way that you might employ an estate agent.

I emailed the agent and someone from her office replied asking for an outline of the book and three sample chapters. He promised to get back to me within two months. Satisfied that I was in good hands, I pressed on. By mid-March I was watching the post daily for a reply. When none came, I emailed again. The following evening, an envelope was lying on the mat when I returned from work. In it was a brief letter from the agent herself, regretting that she could not take me on. Unless she really loved a book, she explained, or identified with it on some deep level, she could not represent the author.

Stunned, I sat down with the letter in my hand. I had heard many stories about manuscripts being rejected by publishers and was totally prepared for that, but it had never occurred to me that one might be rejected by an agent. Now what was I to do? I really didn't think I could face working my way down through the list of agents and being rejected every two months or so. I decided that, in spite of all advice to the contrary, I would take my chances directly with publishers themselves.

So which publishers? That was the next question. My experience with the agent had taught me one thing: the kind of book I had written would not be everyone's meat. I needed to find a publisher who already published that sort of thing. What sort of thing? I wasn't really sure what I had written. It was a memoir, yes, but a quite particular memoir. I realised that the rock I might perish on in the sea of publishing was the fact that there was so much about prayer and spirituality in it. They were not exactly hot topics.

I examined my own bookshelves and came across some other books of a similar genre. In the main, two publishers' names kept cropping up: Hodder & Stoughton and Darton, Longman & Todd. They were both London publishers, but I decided to try them anyway.

The following day was 17 March, St Patrick's Day, so I had a holiday from the office. I despatched an email to the two publishers, explaining that I had written a memoir of a period I had spent with a contemplative community in France in the 1990s. The book, I said, could be described as a sort of spiritual thriller. It described my quest for God, which took the form of both an inner and outer journey, the outer journey leading me to 'Aubépine', the fictitious name I gave to the village where the monastery was situated. The book ended, I went on, with my leaving Aubépine, devastated, yet aware at some deep level that the quest was not yet over and that in spite of all appearances to the contrary, I had not lost my way.

That same evening, to my great surprise and excitement, I received an email from the editorial director of Darton, Longman and Todd, asking to have a look at some sample material. I sent off a synopsis and three chapters and settled in for what I expected would be a long wait. By this time, I had about 40,000 words completed of a projected 50,000.

A week later, DLT was back again, asking to see the rest of the book. It still wasn't finished, but I explained this and sent what I had, trying not to let myself hope.

Weeks passed. I completed the manuscript at the Augustinian Priory in Orlagh, Rathfarnham, where I had gone to spend the three days of Holy Week. In May I went to Glenstal, a Benedictine Abbey in Limerick, where, during a peaceful five days governed by the rhythm of the monks' liturgical life, I reread and revised the entire book. As satisfied as I ever would be, I sent on the entire manuscript to DLT. They said it would be a few months before they would reach a decision; during that time it would go out to external readers for their opinion.

By July, not having heard anything, I emailed DLT with some trepidation and enquired whether it had been put to the firm yet. It seemed to me that this was a case of 'no news is bad news'. Some days passed, and then an email arrived, apologising for the delay. The editorial director had been away for a few days. But he was surprised by my question – he had sent me an email some days previously. It clearly hadn't arrived, so he would send it again straight away. But the news was good! The second email followed. The book had been accepted.

An exciting time followed, as the book went through the various stages of publication and I corrected proofs, made changes and finally saw the cover design and sketches for the illustrations. The book was to be published at the end of March 2005. Early that year came the thrill of receiving the first copies and holding my own book in my hand. All that now remained was actual publication.

The Secret Ladder is an extremely personal story, and it was with some trepidation that I waited to see how friends who had not read the manuscript would react. I was particularly anxious about my colleagues in the Competition Authority. Most of them had no idea that I had spent time in a convent – much less that I had spent time in two convents! Once I knew that the book was going to be published, I told people in the office and of course that involved telling them what the book was about. I was afraid, rather foolishly, that their attitude towards me might change once they knew I had been a nun; that they might feel less comfortable around me. I needn't have had any such fear. Everyone received the news with the greatest of interest, and was full of congratulations about the forthcoming book. It was clear that I was going to sell at least forty copies anyway, as all the colleagues intended to buy it.

Now the friends I worked with knew about my past, but the book was going to teach them much more than that. I had been frank in the book not only about the faults and failings of character and temperament that had led to my departure from Aubépine, but also about my lifelong desire for union with God and about my prayer life. How would workmates react to that?

In fact, the publication of the book was a sort of liberation. People in the office came to talk about what I had written, to ask me questions about it and to express opinions. Never was any opinion a negative one. I felt I could at last really be myself at work, and could freely say, for example, that I was going off to do a retreat during a period of annual leave, or that I was going to visit the nuns in Aubépine rather than, as before, 'going to visit some friends who live in the country in France' – not a lie, certainly, but a statement that created a very different mental image.

I came in for a certain amount of teasing, it's true, but it was very affectionate and it was always based on the shortcomings I had revealed in the book. One episode which I recount in the book relates an epic inner battle that took place over the removal of some old beds from the monastery's attic. I had wrongly believed I had been deliberately not asked to help with this work, and the result had been a fit of pique and the next best thing to a childish tantrum. A few weeks after the book had appeared, the Competition Authority's secretary, Ciaran Quigley, who is a good friend of mine, put his head round the door of my office.

'Noreen,' he said, 'a few of us are going to be bringing down some computers from the fourth floor during the morning. We'll be passing your door here. Is that OK?'

Puzzled, I said it was.

'Would you like to help us?'

Even more perplexed now, I said certainly, if he needed help.

'No,' said Ciaran, 'we don't really need any help, but I thought I'd better mention it all the same, in case you threw a tantrum afterwards ...'

And grinning, he disappeared before I could throw something more solid than a tantrum.

CHAPTER EIGHTEEN

O nymphs of Judaea,
While mid the flowers and rose-trees the ambar sends forth perfume,
Dwell in the outskirts
And desire not to touch our thresholds.

The first two months after the book was published were chaotic – not outwardly, because at first nothing happened at all – but inwardly. My spiritual life suddenly disappeared, or so it seemed to me. Nothing mattered but the book. I discovered in myself a fiercely protective possessiveness where *The Secret Ladder* was concerned. Once it arrived in the shops, I became a compulsive visitor, making daily trips to count how many remained on the shelves from the previous day. The media showed no interest at first. I put this down to the fact that the book was only on sale in the Christian bookstores and I became obsessed with the need to get it into the mainstream shops. After some weeks, the publicity officer pulled off a great coup: she got me an interview on the Marian Finucane Show. This interview generated some attention, and a couple of newspaper interviews followed, as well as a public reading. These small successes fired my enthusiasm even further, and I became even more anxious that the book should be stocked by the high street bookstores. Every day I instituted a Google search for the book to see whether it had been mentioned in any new context since the day before. With anticipation, I opened every letter in my office in-tray, hoping it might contain a request for an interview, or a copy of a review. I could think of nothing else.

As my obsession with sales and with the visibility of the book grew, so my prayer life became more and more difficult. Morning after morning I sat in my prayer room and tried without success to find again the way to the silent secret place. By early June, I felt that I had completely lost the path I had been following. One evening, sitting at dinner after a day in the office,

I was wondering for the umpteenth time how to get back on track. If God would only make some sort of sign ... But of course, he doesn't do that sort of thing very often. Nevertheless, after dinner I went into my prayer room, sat down, took the bible and asked him to point me to a passage that would give me some direction. I opened it at Matthew 12:22:

Then they brought to him a demoniac who was blind and mute; and he cured him, so that the one who had been mute could speak and see.

Well, that's not very helpful, I thought, and was about to close the book and try again. The passage seemed to have absolutely no relevance to where I was. But then something stopped me. I reflected that the word 'gospel' meant 'good news'. Somewhere here there was good news for me. I reminded myself that if I was anxious to get myself back on the path that led to God, God himself must be much more so. This, after all, is the God who goes out searching for the lost sheep and comes back bearing it on his shoulders, calling out to everyone to rejoice with him. John of the Cross puts it in his own way in the *Living Flame of Love*:

If a soul is seeking God, its Beloved is seeking it much more ...

I read the verse again, this time with a short prayer to the Holy Spirit that my heart would be open enough to receive the good news. Suddenly, out of nowhere came the thought: I should talk to Finbarr; I should quite simply tell him exactly what was happening. I looked at my watch; it was 9.30. Was it too late to ring him? I decided to try. I dialled his direct line, and he picked up the phone immediately. I explained to him that all the fuss about the book had un-centred me, and I asked if I could come to see him. We made an appointment for the following Friday. Putting down the phone, I felt a great calm invade me. But I was puzzled. The idea of talking to Finbarr was such a simple one, why had I not thought of it before now? And then it hit me. There was more than one sort of blindness. There was a spiritual as well as a physical one. I had been so blinded by my obsession with book sales that I quite simply had not been able to see what

I should do. Now I understood why I had been directed to that particular gospel passage. I felt suddenly overwhelmed by the nearness of this God who had immediately answered my prayer.

When I went to see Finbarr the following Friday, I understood fully what that gospel passage had meant, because like the man in the gospel passage, I both spoke and saw. As I talked to Finbarr I 'saw' even more what the problem had been. It started with what was almost a chance remark from Finbarr. Having listened to what I had to say, he was musing on what the difficulty might be.

'Prayer for you is essentially a letting-go of control,' he said reflectively. 'In relation to this book business, you've been trying to manage the process …'

Before he had even finished the sentence, realisation dawned on me. My old bogey had returned to haunt me.

Because – I have to admit it – I'm a control freak. It had been one of the major contributions to my inability to live the enclosed way of life at Aubépine. I hadn't felt safe when I wasn't in charge of what was happening. God had tackled this problem at its very core when the nuns told me to leave, and I found myself in an interior wilderness, without any direction. I was forced to let go of control and to learn to trust God instead. Trust is the absolute antithesis of control. When you trust God, you place the control of life and events firmly in his hands. This had been the big insight that the whole Aubépine experience had led me to, and my subsequent relationship with God (including, of course, my prayer life) had been firmly based upon it. From then on I had been vigilant to this tendency in myself, and whenever I found myself attempting to manipulate events or, worse still, other people, I tried to turn to God and make an act of trust instead. It was never easy, but I knew it was essential, and even when I slipped up (as I often did) I got back on track again as quickly as I could. It had seemed to me that I had made a bit of progress in this matter over the past few years, and I was perhaps becoming a little complacent about it. It was time for a shake-up, and that was what all this was about.

Once I saw it, I saw it with total clarity, and the only remaining puzzle was how I could previously have been so blind. There I was, having written the book ostensibly for God's glory in order to tell the story of how he intervenes with love in our lives, and suddenly all I wanted was to be a bestseller! I did all I could to promote sales – a perfectly laudable thing in itself, and indeed I had an obligation to do my part for the sake of the publishers – but I hadn't left it there. I tried to force the publishers themselves and their sales people to do more than they were doing, felt unhappy and aggrieved because I thought they weren't doing enough, obsessed (the badge of the controller!) day and night about it … was it any wonder my prayer life faded away from starvation? Its sustenance had been trust; I had taken away its food and was feeding it with poison.

When I left Finbarr I was newly resolved to leave everything to God. He had done very well without any interference from me up to this. My mind was suddenly free again, and I realised how imprisoned I had been by my anxieties about the book. 'O, the mind, mind, has mountains, cliffs of fall' wrote Gerald Manley Hopkins. We so often create our own prisons, and it often takes someone else to come along and point out to us that the door is actually open, and that we can walk out any time we like.

Ironically – or maybe not; maybe God wanted to make a point – I had no sooner stopped obsessing about the book than people began to take an interest in it. Within a couple of weeks it was reviewed in several periodicals, and I gave some more interviews. Following this, the book became much more visible in the shops. I was delighted by all of this, of course I was, but it was a delight unshadowed by any of the previous anxieties. I realised now that it simply didn't matter whether the book did well or badly; I had told my story, and if it helped one or two people, well, that was enough.

Prayer resumed its former path, but I had learned a valuable lesson. I had to keep my eyes always on the One who was leading me. If I let any other thing replace him in my line of vision, I immediately veered off course. Those eyes engraved in my in-most heart were gazing always upon me; I had to gaze upon them too, or be lost.

CHAPTER NINETEEN

Hide thyself, dearest one,
And look with thy face upon the mountains
And desire not to speak,
But look upon her companions who travels mid strange islands.

After Aubépine, summer holidays began to be a problem. In the old days, my idea of a holiday was to go somewhere warm and sunny, where I could lie on a beach in the mornings, visit places of local and cultural interest in the afternoons, and have dinner in pleasant restaurants in the evenings. But after Aubépine, what I wanted from holidays was, above all, time to pray. I hadn't, however, become so spiritual that prayer was all I wanted. I was well aware of the necessary rest and relaxation that a break from routine and a change of surroundings can bring, but I found it difficult to find places to go where I could combine both. Aubépine itself filled the bill most closely, so I had got into the habit of spending part of my summer holidays there every year.

One year, I tried something different. I had read about an organised trip to Montserrat in Catalonia. The trip was described as a 'spiritual holiday'. The description attracted me. I sent away for a brochure, and learned that it was essentially a package holiday on Montserrat, the 'jagged tooth' mountain, with daily trips to places of interest throughout Catalonia. It was a 'spiritual' holiday because we would be based in a hotel attached to the Benedictine Abbey of Montserrat, and we would be accompanied by Catholic and Anglican chaplains. Mass would be celebrated each day, and evening prayer would be said together. For the rest, the hotel had a restaurant and a bar, and conviviality was encouraged. It sounded delightful, and indeed it was. But when it was over, I didn't think I wanted to do anything similar again. There was a little too much of the package holiday element, and I didn't really like the lack of freedom it implied. That element in my personality which had made it so difficult for me to live in community (or for any community to live with me!) was again at play, and I chafed against the daily organisation of tours and trips to museums. The following year, I resumed my Aubépine routine.

Early in 2005, as people in the office began to discuss holiday plans, I thought again about what it was that I wanted from a holiday. Above all, it was the opportunity to devote myself more fully than was normally possible to the contemplative life. In one way, Aubépine was what I needed. In another, it was not: strange as it may sound, there simply wasn't enough solitude in Aubépine. There were almost always other people staying at the guesthouse, and while that made for interesting meetings, it created an interruption in the solitude that otherwise prevailed. What on earth am I really looking for, I wondered? Then I remembered a chance remark made by a friend at a time when things were not going well in her life.

'I'd love to just go away alone to a cottage in the country,' she had said.

Yes, I thought; that's it. I need a cottage in the country for a couple of weeks.

It wasn't, however, so easy to find one. A search on the internet produced plenty of cottages in the country, but they were either much too big for one person or they were located in areas that were impossible to reach without a car. I have never learned to drive, so it was essential to find somewhere that was accessible by public transport. At last, when I had almost abandoned the idea as impossible, a chance search on Google produced a tiny cottage in the West of Ireland, on the outskirts of a small village. It could be reached by a combination of train and bus, and shops in the village catered for the basic necessities of life. I booked it immediately.

On a glorious Saturday in the last week in August, hot and tired from the journey, I stepped off the bus at the village crossroads and looked around me. The person I had spoken to on the phone had told me the cottage was a five minute walk from the bus stop. I considered my position: one road led back the way I had come, another led towards the mountains, yet another towards the sea. I tossed a mental coin and took the sea road. After a few metres, it petered out into a stony boreen, going uphill. Puffing and panting, I hauled my suitcase-on-wheels over the rough ground. Shades of Aubépine, I thought wryly, remembering my first visit to the monastery when the bus had set me down at dusk in the middle of the countryside and I had been obliged to drag my luggage up a steep hill in the growing darkness, unsure of how far up the monastery was. True to Murphy's Law, it had been at the top.

Fortunately for me, my western cottage was not. Rounding a bend, I saw it on a height above me, white-washed and red-doored as a cottage should be, looking down on a field of sheep. I stopped and leaned on the handle of my suitcase. There it was: my hermitage for the following two weeks. I could feel my soul stretching and expanding at the thought.

Solitude had become increasingly important to me. The prospect of an unbroken stretch of it ahead acted on me now like wine. I was exhilarated. Why was this? Why was it that I saw solitude as a long, clean road, a road that would move me along the journey at speed? I thought again, as at every stage of the journey I was making, of my friend and guide St John of the Cross. His *Spiritual Canticle* mentions solitude more than once, but the verse that always resonated with me was this one:

> In solitude she lived
> And in solitude now has built her nest,
> And in solitude her dear one alone guides her,
> Who likewise in solitude was wounded by love.

Explaining the stanza, John says:

> Inasmuch as the soul has desired to be alone, for the sake of her dear one, and far from all created things, He himself, being enamoured of her because of this her solitariness, has taken care of her, received her into his arms, pastured her in Himself with all blessings and guided her spirit to the high places of God.

Solitude is the path that leads to the solitary place where the Beloved alone is waiting, the place where none appears. It is the place I have been travelling to since I was sixteen, the place where fanning cedars make a breeze that blows from hidden turrets. It is the holy place, the place where lover and Beloved are united, where all ceases. It is the place all of us are searching for, whether we know it or not, even from the womb until now; the place where we will leave our cares forgotten among the lilies.

I began the final slight ascent to the cottage. Bleating sheep rushed in a body to the gate of the field as I approached, apparently thinking it was feeding time. Feeling a little guilty, I ignored them and pressed on. They fell silent. Looking back, I saw them standing motionless, their heads turning in unison to follow my disappearing back, the picture of stoical disappointment.

I arrived at the cottage. The front door was locked, apparently bolted from within. I went around to the back and entered that way. I was in a small tiled lobby leading into the kitchen. The door from the kitchen to the living room was open; I went through. A sense of deja-vu possessed me: I was back in Aubépine. There was the pine dresser; there were the raftered ceiling, the white walls and the oil-cloth-covered table of the *hôtellerie*. Taking a deep breath, I dropped my bags and sank down on the sofa. (Well, that was one difference anyway. There hadn't been any sofas in Aubépine!) As the first shock faded, I saw that despite some striking similarities, it was really quite different. I was in an old cottage living room, dominated by a huge open fireplace. The television set in the corner was not an item I had ever seen in the monastery either. The floor was made of huge stone flags, and the furniture was simple and basic – the sofa I was sitting on, the dresser, a couple of chairs and the big table. There were three small windows, two on one side and one on the other. Beside the single window was the front door. Getting up, I crossed over and examined it. It was a half door. Unbolting the top half, I opened it and looked out. I was looking down on the little road I had travelled from the bus. There were my friends the sheep, who appeared to have already forgotten me and who were busy once more about their sheeply business of standing around like toy models. In the distance, golden in the late afternoon sun, the yellow stone of an old church lent a timeless quality to the scene. Overhead, a few small wispy clouds hung motionless in the still air. Everything in me relaxed. This was really getting away from it all. I leant on the half door like an old woman of the nineteenth century and breathed in the peace.

The next day, I established my hermit's routine. (A rather self-indulgent hermit, it must be admitted; one who had a lie-in every morning and enjoyed a glass of wine with her evening meal. But I was, after all, a hermit on holiday.) After breakfast, I strolled up the boreen to the village to buy the paper. From there it was just a few steps to the parish church which, unlike churches in Dublin, remained open all day. There I recited Morning Prayer of the Divine Office, and stayed there for an hour or so before wandering back to the cottage to read the paper. Afternoons were spent writing, then there was just time for a short walk before reciting evening prayer and attending Mass which, most days, took place at 7.30 in the evening. Then it was back to the cottage for a simple meal of fresh vegetables and a piece of chicken or a chop, and so to bed.

A few days of this routine infused my mind and body with a sense of wellbeing. On the fifth day, Mary Flannery, a barrister friend from Dublin, came down for a few days. She had a car, and this opened up the countryside to me. I took a few days off from my hermit existence and became a tourist with Mary.

The first day, we drove to Roonagh Pier and took the ferry to Clare Island, an island of some 150 inhabitants situated at the mouth of Clew Bay. On the boat, we kept watch hopefully for the dolphins which often accompany the ferry, but they were not abroad that day. It didn't matter. With the wind in our hair and the sun on the sea, we bounced gloriously across the Atlantic to the island harbour.

On the island, we had a quick look at the stronghold of the sixteenth century pirate queen Grace O'Malley – or Gráineuaile, as she is known in Ireland – which is perched on a height over-looking the bay. Married to a sixteenth century chieftain, Gráineuaile took charge of her husband's men when he was murdered by a rival clan. She established herself on Clare Island from where she made forays out to sea to attack cargo vessels. In 1593, when the English viceroy in Ireland began suppressing local chieftains, she visited London where she had an audience with Queen Elizabeth I, who granted her protection and gave her the right to live out her days in peace.

Leaving Graineuaile's castle, Mary and I set off across coun-try for a long tramp which brought us past a ruined Cistercian abbey and finally led us, after some hours, back to the harbour in time to catch the ferry back to the mainland.

Another day, we went to the Céide Fields, the most extensive stone-age field system in Europe. On the way back, we visited another island, Achill. The scenery there is very different from the quiet pastoral landscape of Clare Island. Achill, beloved of painters, poets and mystics, is full of dramatic cliffs, brooding waters and shifting light patterns. We arrived there in the early evening when the light was at its most wonderful. Driving northwards across the island we came at last to Dugort in the shadow of Slievemore. The dark mountain loomed over the water and as we approached it, I fell silent, aware again of that presence I had felt so many years earlier in Piperstown in the Dublin hills.

At Dugort, we found what we had set out to look for: McDowell's Hotel. Mary had stayed there once with her late husband, and had happy memories of the little inn set right into the lowest slopes of Slievemore. For me, going there was a sort of pilgrimage in homage to one of the most charismatic teachers I have ever known, Moira McDowell.

Mrs McDowell was the Miss Jean Brodie of my schooldays. In 1961, she arrived to teach Latin, French and German at the Holy Faith Convent in the Coombe, Dublin, where I was then in third year. She was at that time in her fifties, with an invalid husband and two teenage sons. The day she walked into our French class, I was thrilled. Prematurely white-haired, small and rotund, she was Mademoiselle from Enid Blyton's *Malory Towers* books to the life.

She was great fun. From fifth year onwards, she was our Latin teacher. Only five girls in my class were studying Latin, so we had to vacate our regular classroom and find whatever empty room was available. With Mrs McDowell at our head we would parade the corridors until we found a room, chanting loudly 'Here come the wanderers, no fixed abode!' She taught us Latin by the simple expedient of getting us to translate the prescriptions the doctor had written for her husband, and by translating pop songs into Latin for us.

After I had left school I went to her for private Latin classes, in preparation for my entrance into the Carmelite monastery of Firhouse. The Divine Office was recited in Latin in those days, and the prioress thought it would be a good idea for me to improve my knowledge of the language. So it was that every Monday evening I took the bus to the chaotic old house in Terenure, where, with her usual flare for improvisation, Mrs McDowell abandoned the prescriptions and the pop songs, and set me to translating the psalms in the breviary.

While I was in Firhouse, she had visited me regularly, and after I left we continued our friendship. Following her retirement from teaching, she taught English to Spanish and Italian Franciscan novices who were spending their summer at the friary in Merchant's Quay in Dublin. One evening, she phoned me to say that the Superior in Merchant's Quay had asked her to oblige him by bringing the young Franciscans on some sort of cultural outing typical of Dublin. He left the nature of the cultural event up to her. She had given some thought to the matter, she told me, and had now decided what to do. Would I come along to help? Certainly, I said, what were we going to do?

We were going to go on a pub crawl, said Mrs McDowell firmly. It was a night to remember, and many of the Franciscan students found, under the influence of Guinness, a fluency in the English language neither Mrs McDowell nor they had known they possessed.

At her 80th birthday party, at which I was present, she made a speech in which she wished that all of us might also reach 80, so long as we were, like her, mobile, *compos mentis* and continent. She died while I was in Aubépine, so I had not been able to attend her funeral. She had often, during her lifetime, spoken to me of her husband's sister, Elizabeth, who she greatly loved. Elizabeth lived on Achill where the family ran a small hotel, and Mrs McDowell visited her there often. It was in memory of that great teacher and friend that I now stood in the small front garden of the little hotel, thinking of her with deep affection.

The hotel was no longer owned by the McDowell family, but it had retained the name. Mary and I decided to eat there at a table looking out over the fields. During the meal, a solitary sheep strolled down the road in a nonchalant manner. We ate chicken and fresh peas and drank a glass of mellow red wine. It was late when we set off on the long drive back to the cottage, and Slievemore was brooding darkly over the valley. Back in the cottage, we lit a fire and sat talking until it was late.

A few days later, after Mary had left, I visited another mountain, Croagh Patrick in Murrisk. This was the mountain on which St Patrick was said to have passed forty days and forty nights in prayer; it has been a place of pilgrimage for over a thousand years. Cone shaped and rocky, its peak is often hidden in the clouds, but when I arrived at its base, the entire mountain was majestically visible. The day was unusually hot for an Irish September and black clouds behind the mountain made an ominous backdrop. There were climbers all over the mountain, but none of those I met were Irish. I wondered whether they were climbing for religious reasons or whether it had simply become another tourist thing to do.

I climbed a short distance up the lower slopes and recited evening prayer sitting on a rock. It was appropriate: the mountain was a place of prayer. I remembered that the gospels tell us that Jesus sometimes climbed a mountain to pray, and sitting there in the solitude, I understood why. There was something holy about those ancient high places. Many of the great epiphanies took place on mountains: Moses received the tablets of stone engraved with the ten commandments upon a mountain; it was on a mountain that the prophet Elijah stood while God passed by in the whisper of a gentle breeze, and it was on another mountain that Jesus was transfigured in the sight of Peter, James and John.

I got up and went into the visitors' centre. The café there was filled with German climbers who had just completed the climb. They were in great humour. They cheered everyone who came into the restaurant. They cheered me, under the impression that I, too, had made the climb. I bowed and acknowledged the applause and didn't enlighten them. I drank coffee and ate scones and jam and wrote postcards. I was, after all, on holiday.

Later, still filled with the silence of the mountain, I walked through the ruins of Murrisk Abbey. From its graveyard, you could see on one side the sea washing up on a stony beach, and on the other, Croagh Patrick.

The holiday had been one of islands and mountains. In John of the Cross' poem, the searcher who has seen the eyes desired on the silvered surface of the crystal fountain goes on to describe how after that experience, she found her Beloved in those remote places:

My Beloved, the mountains, the solitary wooded valleys,
The strange islands, the sonorous rivers, the whisper of the amorous breezes

Those western islands and mountains haunted me. I seemed to see Slievemore especially in my dreams, standing dark and immutable over the waters of Dugort. Achill was full of mystery. It spoke to me of the desired eyes that I once saw. Its beauty left an ache in my heart and something there was calling me back. It was perhaps Achill that prepared my soul for the next experience I was to have of God.

CHAPTER TWENTY

Let us rejoice, Beloved,
And let us go to see ourselves in thy beauty,
To the mountain or the hill where flows the pure water;
Let us enter further into the thicket.

And then we shall go forth
To the lofty caverns of the rock which are well hidden,
And there shall we enter
And taste the new wine of the pomegranates.

Holidays cannot last forever. The end was in sight, and I tried hard not to feel that it had already come as I started to clean up the cottage and pack away my belongings in preparation for departure the following day. A difficulty in remaining in the present moment was, I knew, one of my many failings. I was always catching myself out in the act of leaping ahead in anticipation of what was to come: a pleasant enough activity when you were looking forward to something, but the knell of death when you were not. At such times, it was a destroyer of present joys. I played little tricks with myself: I tried to tell myself that tomorrow might never come, but I didn't really believe it, even though it wouldn't come for millions of people all over the world, some of whom, like me, were also wishing it would not. Or I pretended that I had just come down for the day, and so, instead of a day of departure, it was a day of arrival. But these were all games, I knew that. The reality was that the present moment is all we ever possess, so it is sensible and right to make all we can of it.

So what was the present moment, there in that little cottage towards which I had such proprietary feelings, even after only two weeks? The fine weather had at last broken and my last day was wet, cold and windy. I had gone to the shop and bought a colourful looking bag called a Firepak, which you put into your fire grate, wrapping and all, and just set a match to it. In this way, you could make a blazing fire without any trouble at all. I wished I had known earlier in the fortnight about this admirable invention. There had been one or two chilly evenings when I had attempted to light a fire with the peat briquettes kindly left for me by the landlord. It had not been a success. In spite of much newspaper, rolled and knotted in the way my mother used to do it, and the addition of half a packet of Zip firelighters, the fire, after an initially impressive showing due solely, I afterwards realised, to the firelighters, had always settled down to a dull smouldering, generating neither heat nor cheerfulness. The excellent Firepak, on the other hand, blazed away merrily, and when it died down a little I only had to give it a gentle poke with the rather unwieldy tongs and up it flared again, just like a proper fire.

I don't know what John of the Cross would have made of Firepaks. It would have been difficult to use them as metaphors for the love of God burning away the dross until the dross itself became fire. The Firepak (and I was second to none in my admiration for it) did none of the things that John found so useful when describing the properties of burning wood. It emitted no odours; no noxious creatures came crawling forth from it, and worst of all, it did not, in the end, glow with the very fire itself. It simply disintegrated economically into a pile of sooty-looking ash which I shovelled up and placed in the ash-bucket outside the back door.

But the bad weather and the fire were a great help in keeping me in the present moment. Apart from a trip to the church for Mass (that day was one of the few weekdays when Mass was in the morning) I was content, having cleaned and packed and inspected the now shining kitchen, to sit by the fire with my laptop on my knee and write. If the day had been fine, I would have felt obliged at least to go out for a walk. Happily reprieved, and with no sense of guilt, I felt the day stretch itself out, and the morrow no longer seemed to have already arrived. I had all afternoon, all evening and all night before me. When I had finished writing for the day, I drew the curtains and said evening prayer. Then I lowered the lights and made my way to that trysting place where I knew there was always someone waiting, even if I did not see him. Even if he did not reveal again his eyes, I knew they were engraved on my inmost heart. There they watched me continually with their loving gaze. Such constant watchfulness was in no way threatening. Instead it brought calm and peace, for I knew that those eyes saw everything, my failures as well as my successes, and that their loving gaze never faltered.

The crystal fountain experience had been an experience of God present within me. Paradoxically, we are also present in God, in whom we live, move and have our being. I knew this in my head, but I hadn't yet experienced it in my heart. In Piperstown in the Dublin hills, at the age of sixteen, I had experienced a sense of the presence of God, but it was a presence that was in some way separate from and outside of me and of everything else. I felt the presence of God that day in the same way that I might feel the presence of someone who had just come into a dark room. God was in that place, not of it. I was now to discover for myself that God is not separate from everything else, and neither are we. And if we are not separate from everything else, then we are not separate from one another; we are all part of one another, and in that truth lies the most enormous responsibility.

It was early winter. I was on my way to Luxembourg to attend a legal conference and instead of flying direct from Dublin, I had taken the longer but much cheaper option of flying to Charleroi in Belgium and travelling on by train. At Charleroi airport, I had a long wait in freezing weather for the bus to the railway station. By the time I got on the train that was to bring me from Charleroi to Namur, I was cold and miserable and thinking longingly of my hotel, of a hot bath and a meal.

I had a window seat, and was gazing idly out at the passing scenery when without any warning there was a sudden shift in my consciousness. I remember that I was looking at the time at an outcrop of rock when it became invested with extraordinary significance. Astonished, I tore my gaze away. My eyes fastened on a clump of trees crowning a distant hill. They suddenly thrilled me. Then a little stony path through a field filled me with delight. It was like the dawn chorus, when first one bird, then two and then every bird within hearing begins to pour out its heart, only here the music was coming from all creation. One by one, hills, rivers, trees, stones rose up and began to sing. Everything was one and everything was in One, and I was caught up in it all somewhere … for I was no longer aware of myself as in any way separate from the paean of praise that was pouring out all around me. Every bush was burning, the hills leaped like rams before the Lord of heaven and earth; the morning stars sang together and all heavenly beings shouted for joy.

I left the train at Namur to change for Luxembourg. I was bewildered and intoxicated. It can't continue, I thought; it's too good to be true. But all the way to Luxembourg the great symphony went on. As the train climbed through the Ardennes we reached the snowline and I had never seen snow like this before, snow which so exulted in its snow-ness. Everything was in its rightful place and everything rejoiced to be there. The Beloved had revealed his eyes to all his creation. He had looked at them as he passed and by his glance alone left them clothed in beauty.

But insight into the truth of things cannot be all joy. Seeing the truth while we still live on earth has to imply seeing into the pain that is also inherent in creation in its present imperfect state.

> For the creation waits with eager longing for the revealing of the children of God; for the creation was subjected to futility, not of its own will but by the will of the one who subjected it, in hope that the creation itself will be set free from its bondage to decay and obtain the freedom of the glory of the children of God. We know that the whole creation has been groaning in labour pains until now, and not only the creation, but we ourselves who have the first fruits of the Spirit, groan inwardly while we wait for adoption, the redemption of our bodies. *(Romans 8:20-23)*

Some door had been opened in my heart that had allowed me to see into the joyful heart of creation; through the same door, I could not but also see its pain, as I discovered a few weeks later.

It was around seven o'clock on a bitterly cold evening, and as I was making my way along O'Connell Street towards my bus and home, I saw a man standing at the corner of Abbey Street. I had almost passed him when I realised he had said something in such a low tone that, preoccupied with my own concerns, I had hardly heard him at all. I stopped and looked at him. He spoke again:

'Could you spare some change for a hostel?'

I pulled a few euros from my pocket and went over to him.

'Would you believe,' he said, 'you're the first person who has stopped, and I've been here for two hours.'

I was horrified. Looking at him more closely, I saw that he was shivering. He had been standing there hopelessly in a sub-zero temperature, and nobody had stopped. Putting the coins back in my pocket, I took out my purse, found a note and handed it to him.

He looked at the note, saw it was a twenty and handed it back to me. He thought I had made a mistake. He was giving me back the money that I didn't need, but that would have fed him and got him a bed for the night. I felt pierced through.

'No,' I said, 'It's for you. Please take it and go and get a hot meal.'

He took it then, and looked at me with such a depth of misery, disbelief and thanks that I could hardly bear it. I wanted to take him into my arms and protect him there from any more pain. Instead, I said goodnight and went home to my own warm comfortable home. But that inner door had been opened again, and I had once more seen into the truth of things. This time, the pain was as deep as the joy had been before.

CHAPTER TWENTY-ONE

There wouldst thou show me
That which my soul desired,
And there at once, my life, wouldst thou give me
That which thou gavest me the other day.

The breathing of the air,
The song of the sweet philomel,
The grove and its beauty in the serene night,
With a flame that consumes and gives no pain.

There is very little left to tell, although I have no doubt that the story is far from over. I am writing these final words in Aubépine itself, for it is September again and I am back here for a week of my summer holidays.

Many years have passed since I left Aubépine and since the events recounted in the early chapters of this book. The September weather is identical with the weather of that year: warm and golden days and nights cool enough to be able to pull up the blanket and sleep well. Perfect weather.

I have not come alone: Maeve Kerney, with whom I began the prayer group in my parish at home, is with me. It is Maeve's second trip to Aubépine, which is now a place whose spiritual resources I want to share with my friends.

This morning, before the sun had reached its full strength, we set off on the three-kilometre walk to the village of Aubépine. I wanted to visit the graves of the sisters with whom I had lived during that year and a half, and who have since died. They are buried in the local cemetery, a small and simple place on a hillside, in the shadow of a twelfth-century church.

We make our way from the monastery down the hill that I had climbed so laboriously on my first ever visit to Aubépine in 1994, passing the farm half way down, and admiring a field of yellow sunflowers which had not been there at that time. We come across more plantations of sunflowers as we turn onto the road leading to the village: tall floppy heads twisted this way and that, looking almost human, like flowers in a children's fairy story; lacking only eyes and smiling mouths.

At the village, we climb the small ascent to the cemetery and make our way through imposing marble monuments until we reach the quiet patch, a little apart from the other graves, where, marked by simple wooden crosses, the bodies of some of my friends lie. I go first to Annette's grave, dear Annette, who was the first of the Aubépine community to be my friend, Annette who used to call me her *'Grande Fidèle'*, because I came so often – and because I was tall. It was Annette who had charge of the *hôtellerie* during those early years, and her death has left a gap in my heart and in the heart of the community. I tell Maeve a little about her, about how she loved her other job as sacristan, and how, if you were looking for her during her time off from the *hôtellerie*, you would almost invariably find her sitting in her tiny sacristy, sewing altar linens and praying.

Then we move on to the grave beside Annette's; this is where Marie-Cécile is lying, that valiant old warrior who, from her wheelchair, fought a losing battle against arthritis. I reminded Maeve that it was when demonstrating a six-hand reel at Marie-Cécile's golden jubilee that I had torn my Achilles tendon in two, necessitating a week-long stay in hospital.

We stand in silence for a while in that still, sunlit place, listening to the bees and the crickets. A hawk soars far above our heads, and comes to land on the steeple of the old church. I look around at the cluster of Aubépine graves and think how there is another Aubépine community somewhere, in that unimaginable place where we will all meet again some day. Perhaps when that day comes, I will be able to join the Aubépine community again, this time forever, because those human weaknesses which made it impossible for me to live in the community here on earth will have been healed and swept away. 'Behold, I make all things new' says the One who sits on the throne, in the Book of Revelations. And he adds 'These words are certain and true.'

But for the moment, although Aubépine can never be my physical home, it is always the place of my spiritual belonging. I come back here with a sense of homecoming, although I am always conscious that the peace I feel when I visit here was singularly lacking during the year and a half that I lived here.

There is a young woman staying in the *hôtellerie* who is quite clearly a prospective postulant, although she hasn't volunteered that information. But I can recognise a would-be member of the community a mile away. There is something about the way she makes herself at home in the guesthouse, preparing the table for meals and organising the cleaning up, and the way she takes out a prayer stool in the chapel so that she can pray in the same physical attitude as the nuns, instead of sitting up in the benches like the rest of us. And just now, I looked out my window and saw her making her way through the garden trundling a wheelbarrow, clearly on route to weeding the irises. I have seen other postulants at the same task – indeed, I have done it myself. I look at her; she seems to be in her late twenties. She is tall, with long, light-brown hair swept back from a wide forehead and falling down her back in a thick plait. She looks happy. I wonder a little about her; what her history is, how she came to know the community at Aubépine. I hope everything works out for her – by which I mean that I hope her own plans for herself are the same as God's plans for her. If they are, she will be very happy; if they are not, she will have a long struggle ahead of her, but if she can bring herself to let go of what she believes to be in her own best interests and embrace with total trust what God has in store for her, she will find riches beyond belief, just as I have. She will find those eyes desired, the eyes of the One she is seeking, hidden in the depths of her own heart. That is the pearl of great price; that is the treasure hidden in the field. The one who finds that has found everything, whether that person is a nun of Aubépine or a lawyer working for the Competition Authority, or a parent, or a homeless person.

Eight years ago, I could not have borne to watch that young woman, full of hopes for the future, when my own had, as I thought, been crushed and killed. I would have resented her, I would secretly have hoped that she too would find herself unable to live with the community. Someone else's failure would at that time have made me feel a lot better about my own. I remember how I kept secretly hoping, during the first months after my departure, that I would hear that Angèle, my old companion of the novitiate, had also left. That would have been a slap in the eye for Marie-Jeanne and Véronique, I used to think. But as the months went by, and Angèle, far from leaving, began to positively blossom, I realised how a way of life that would have destroyed me as a human being was for her the means of development and, as the French would say, *épanouissement*. For Angèle is no longer the shy, rather repressed girl that I knew in the novitiate. She is now an attractive, confident woman, who greets me, as she did on my arrival last night, with the delight and affection of an old friend. She is flourishing in the soil in which God has planted her. I would have withered there.

Coming out of the chapel after evening prayer, I am approached by a tall, raw-boned middle-aged woman who addresses me in halting French, with a heavy German accent. She is strangely garbed. She is wearing a faded blue denim dress of an unfashionable length, just below the knee. On her head is a sort of headscarf, blue and white, tied in gypsy fashion. She is very sunburnt. She wishes to see one of the sisters, she explains. I tell her she cannot, that visiting time ends at 4.45, that she will have to return another day. She is taken aback; the sisters are expecting her, she says. She and her friend are coming to stay at the guesthouse. I lead her into the *hôtellerie*, where her friend is waiting. The friend is small and dark-haired and is wearing a tee-shirt and rather long navy shorts. They are like Mutt and Jeff, I think. We all climb the stairs and examine the doors of the bedrooms. Sure enough, one of them has a little white Post-it stuck to it. '*Deux soeurs allemandes*', it says. I ask them if they are two German sisters. The tall one says they are not, but that they are two German friends. We conclude that the room, which has two beds in it, must be for them. They go back down to bring up their rucksacks, and I tell them slowly and carefully that they must be downstairs at 7.20 for the evening meal, and that they

will see one of the sisters then. I know that Angèle will be serv-
ing the meal. The small woman speaks no French. The tall one is
anxious to ensure that they have properly understood the time
of the meal, and I show her the hands on my watch, like teaching
a child the time.

At supper time, the two are in the *salle*, hovering awkwardly
by the table. Angèle arrives and shakes hands with them, and
they exchange a few words. The tall woman says they will be
leaving early the next morning. Then the rest of the guests arrive. Apart from the young woman who might be a postulant,
there are two young nuns wearing very unusual long flowing
black habits and short white veils. They have not spoken since
Maeve and I have arrived, neither has the young woman. All
meals so far have been taken in total silence. Meals in the *hôtellerie* are not always totally silent. Sometimes people are happy to
talk a little bit, but even if they prefer complete silence, it is a
tradition that some conversation takes place at coffee after the
midday meal. Those who wish to keep silence can take the coffee to their rooms. However, the present group had all taken coffee at the table, and the silence remained unbroken. Neither
Maeve nor I had felt able to do anything about it.

The tall German woman has no such inhibition. She joins me
at the side table where I am cutting chunks off the long baguette
for everyone; she has a map in her hand. She talks loudly, if halt-
ingly. Her name, she says, is Christiane. She tells me that she
and her friend are on pilgrimage to Compostella. They are on
foot, and they have made a detour to visit Aubépine, because
she had spent a week there once, and wanted her friend to see it.
She asks me to help her plan out their route for the following
day. I tell her firmly that she couldn't have asked a worse person. I am so lacking in any basic sense of direction that I have
more than once got lost in the building where the Competition
Authority has its offices. If I were to attempt to direct her on her
way, I tell her, she is more likely to end up in Australia than in
Cluny, which is their next port of call. I turn to my fellow guests
to enlist their help, although I have some doubts as to whether

any of them can speak at all. I have never met such a totally silent bunch of guests. However, the pilgrims' dilemma gets everyone talking. We all consult the map, and finally an acceptable route is plotted. The young woman asks Christiane if the clothes she is wearing are a religious habit. Christiane says they are. She is a hermit, she explains. She belongs to a newly formed congregation of hermits in Germany. Each lives alone, but twice a year they spend an entire week together. For the rest, their time is divided between prayer, parish work, and earning their own living, for, being hermits, they do not have goods in common and do not mutually support each other financially.

The arrival of the pilgrims has broken the ice and soon we are all introducing ourselves. Christiane's friend, a married woman and mother of three grown-up children, is Caritas. The young woman is Hélène. The nuns turn out to be from an Orthodox community, and are called Sister Barbara and Sister Gabrielle. Neither of them is French. Sister Barbara is Belgian and Sister Gabrielle is German. With cries of delight, Christiane and Caritas immediately break into their own language. Sister Gabrielle replies rather reluctantly. Then everyone speaks French again. It is liked the United Nations, I say. We all laugh.

Christiane is astonished that we have all been together for two days and haven't introduced ourselves until now. Sister Barbara, who now turns out to be the livelier of the two nuns, says that we have been observing silence. She is dark and pretty and very young. She has a smile that lights up her face. Christiane is embarrassed, she is afraid they have disturbed everyone. I rush to reassure her.

'We needed a hermit to come to get us talking', Sister Barbara says, and we all laugh again. Now we are all much more relaxed. People ask Maeve and me where we come from. Sister Barbara, amazingly, tells us that she has studied at UCD, on an Erasmus scholarship. She loved Ireland, but found life on campus disappointing. She had expected everyone to be playing Irish traditional music all day. She would love to have gone to Trinity, she says, and is delighted when Maeve tells her that she had gone there.

I look at the two German women. They are about my own age, but they have the kind of courage I totally lack. I wish I could decide to do a pilgrimage to Compostella, but I know I would be beset by fears. I would be afraid of exhaustion, of staying in uncomfortable places, of having to share rooms with strangers. I realise, not for the first time, how much my life is controlled and my freedom restricted by fears. It is one of my many weaknesses, and one of the things that I am sure blocks my journey onwards. It is the many-headed dragon that must be slain before I can get to the place of heart's desire. My holiday in the West of Ireland made that very clear to me. When I was in my little cottage on the edge of the Atlantic, I could get to the sea in five minutes by walking up a hill at the back of the cottage. There was a beach at the other side of the hill. Four times, I set out to walk to that beach. Four times I turned back half way, because a black farm dog stood in the middle of the road barking at me. I am inordinately afraid of dogs, among the litany of other things I am inordinately afraid of: illness, things happening to people I love, throwing up, flying, riding a bicycle, driving a car, darkness, travelling in underground trains, heights …

So when that dog barked at me, and I turned back, I knew two things: I knew that my fear of dogs was restricting my freedom to go to the beach, and I knew that fear itself was something that was not consistent with total trust in God. And without total trust in God, how could I ever reach the secret place? Perfect love casts out fear. The secret place is the place of perfect love. Perhaps the answer lies in the very conundrum, like an eastern koan. Perhaps the fear will only be cast out when I get to the place I cannot get to while I am still afraid. Whatever the answer, the way is clear. The way has to be trust, and I know this is the lesson that God has been teaching me from the time I left Aubépine even until now.

And so I sit here this evening in Aubépine, that place of many memories, and I think about these things. I think how God has never left me alone, and I think of the morning when I knew he was always with me, closer to me than my own essence, the morning that the crystal fountain yielded up its secrets. Remembering this, I wonder why it is that I minded so much when my cottage holiday ended last year, since the trysting-place goes with me wherever I go. Perhaps it is because I seem so often in these past years to have to leave places that I love: my apartment in Luxembourg, Aubépine, Mariners Court, that little house on the Atlantic seaboard. But then I remind myself that this is the nature of a quest. For a quest is, after all, a journey. One must always be saying, no, it is not here, I must go further.

I am in good company. I think of the pilgrim that I met in Chambarand. He too, like all pilgrims throughout the ages is searching for something, for someone. I wonder where he is tonight and I hope he has found a bed. I think of Lydia, the Little Sister of Jesus, wandering the roads of Europe in her literal living out of the gospel.

> Pilgrimage is a way of projecting our inner and unmanageable hopes, longings, bewilderments, fears and confusions into an outer and more manageable form. We choose some objective that represents the unidentifiable longing of the inner self. For pilgrims, the objective is the holy place to which they have decided to go. We set out on our journey and subsequent decisions are ultimately determined by the desire to reach our destination. We may think that the sole purpose of the journey is to reach our chosen destination, but, at a deeper level, we are also setting out in order to reach a better understanding of the inner journey that we embark on at conception and complete at the moment of death.
> (Gerard Hughes, *God in All Things*)

And on all such journeys, there are Rivendells, places of rest where we can refresh ourselves before going on further, places of music and light and peace. But beautiful and seductive as those places may be, we must eventually, like Frodo, move on; for they are not *that* Place, the place where he awaits, the 'place where none appeared.'

There, (says John of the Cross) he stayed sleeping.

But if he is sleeping, how will I see his eyes, those eyes which I once saw, and long to see again? Perhaps I will not need to. I look again at the last verse of John's poem, *The Dark Night*:

There he stayed sleeping, and I caressed him,
and the fanning of the cedars made a breeze.
The breeze blew from the turrets as I parted his locks;
with his gentle hand he wounded my neck
and caused all my senses to be suspended.
I remained, lost in oblivion;
my face I reclined on the Beloved.
All ceased and I abandoned myself,
leaving my cares forgotten among the lilies.